D0833742

Insects &
Spiders

Insects &
Spiders

CONSULTANT EDITOR
Dan Bickel

FOG CITY PRESS

Published by Fog City Press
814 Montgomery Street
San Francisco, CA 94133 USA

WELDON OWEN PTY LTD
Chief Executive Officer John Owen
President Terry Newell
Publisher Lynn Humphries
Managing Editor Janine Flew
Art Director Kylie Mulquin
Editorial Coordinator Tracey Gibson
Editorial Assistants Marney Richardson, Kiren Thandi
Production Manager Martha Malic-Chavez
Business Manager Emily Jahn
Vice President International Sales Stuart Laurence
European Sales Director Vanessa Mori

LIMELIGHT PRESS PTY LTD
Project Management Jayne Denshire
Project Editor Helen Cooney
Designer Avril Makula
Picture Researcher Annette Crueger
Consultant Editor Dan Bickel

ISBN 1 876778 84 9

Color reproduction by Colourscan Co Pte Ltd
Printed by LeeFung-Asco Printers
Printed in China

A Weldon Owen Production

Welcome to the
Home Reference Library

We have created this exciting new series of books with the help of an international team of consultants, writers, editors, photographers, and illustrators, all of whom share our common vision—the desire to convey our passion and enthusiasm for the natural world through books that are enjoyable to read, authoritative as a source of reference, and fun to collect.

Finding out about things *should* be fun. That's the basic premise of the *Home Reference Library*. So, we've ensured that every picture tells a story, every caption encapsulates a fascinating fact, and every paragraph contains useful or interesting information.

It is said that seeing is believing. We believe seeing is understanding, too. That's why in the *Home Reference Library* we have combined text and images in an imaginative, dynamic design style that conveys the excitement of finding out about the natural world. Cut-away cross-sections detail the inner workings of a termite mound or the 2,000-million-year-old rock strata of the Grand Canyon. Photographs reveal extraordinary facts about the minutest forms of animal life, aspects of the behavior of nature's fiercest predators, or the beauty of a world far beyond our planet.

Each handy-sized book is a complete source of reference on its subject. Collect all the titles in the *Home Reference Library* series to compile an invaluable encyclopedic resource that you'll return to again and again.

From the editors of the *Home Reference Library*.

Nature, in her blind search for life, has filled every possible cranny of the Earth with some sort of fantastic creature!

Joseph Wood Krutch (1893–1970),
American critic and naturalist

CONTENTS

A WORLD OF INSECTS AND SPIDERS

An insight into the secret lives
of these extraordinary creatures

Understanding Insects and Spiders

WITH MORE THAN A MILLION species worldwide, and
many more to be identified, insects and spiders are the
most numerous and successful creatures on our planet.
In fact, they outnumber all other animal species combined.
The study of insect and spider evolution, classification,
and anatomy leads us to a greater knowledge of these
endlessly fascinating animals—and ultimately to
a better understanding of our world.

INSECT AND SPIDER ORIGINS

I nsects and spiders first appeared on the Earth during the early Devonian period, but no one is really sure how they evolved. This is because there are relatively few fossilized specimens. We do know, however, that they had begun to colonize the continents long before vertebrates struggled onto land.

DELICATE LEGACY

Despite their abundance, insects and spiders rarely became fossils because of the delicate nature of their exoskeleton and muscle tissue. The fossilized insect specimens that have been found are very often badly crushed. But the study of early fossil arthropods has allowed scientists to draw some conclusions. The first insects may have evolved from centipede-like ancestors. There is evidence that the earliest fossil scorpions, which are related to spiders, date back about 425 million years. Some were amphibious "giants," measuring more than 3 feet (1 m) long. Fossils do confirm that land-based insects were flourishing about 395 million years ago.

Age of flowers During the Carboniferous Period, about 360 to 285 million years ago, many new species of arthropod emerged to exploit every inch of the humid forests. By 300 million years ago, diverse groups had developed new equipment and techniques to feed on different plant parts.

Insects continued to adapt to environmental forces. One force was the evolution of flowering plants, or angiosperms. This food supply enhanced the chances of survival of any creature that could exploit it. Many insects developed the ability to see wavelengths of light invisible to other animals, enabling them to find pollen and nectar more easily.

On the wing By far, the most important development for insects was the ability to fly. Insects could move to new and varied environments and to the new and sometimes abundant food sources that angiosperms provided. The plants also took advantage of this mobility, rewarding insects with nectar to spread their pollen over great distances.

AMBER AND STONE

Amber, or fossilized tree resin, contains the best examples of ancient insects and spiders. Delicate insect hairs and even DNA fragments are preserved (above). Fine-grain shale can yield beautiful specimens, such as this snakefly (right).

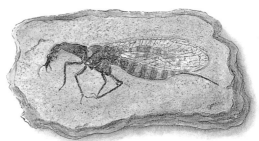

HARD CASES

Insects and spiders belong to a group of animals called arthropods (from the Greek word *arthropoda*, meaning "jointed legs"), which also includes scorpions, ticks, crabs, and centipedes. One thing that all these creatures have in common is a tough outer skeleton covering the whole body. This is called an exoskeleton, or cuticle, and it is made from a material called chitin. This substance is remarkably light yet incredibly strong. Insect and spider muscles are attached to the appendages and the body wall in such a way that great strength in relation to size results. Ants, for example, can carry many times their own body weight in their mandibles.

Shedding skin In order to grow to adult size and shape, and because their cuticle is relatively inflexible, arthropods shed their old exoskeleton and replace it with a new, larger one at regular intervals. Some insects molt only twice in their lifetime, whereas others molt more than 25 times.

NEW SKIN Spiders molt their old skin to grow to a new size. Timing is important; if the weather is too dry, the spider gets stuck in the old exoskeleton and dies.

1 A spider hangs from its web as its old exoskeleton splits along the edge of the cephalothorax.

2 The old skin covering its abdomen comes away as it tries to pull its legs free.

3 The spider expands to its new size while its exoskeleton is soft. The new skin takes 20 minutes to dry.

CICADA EMERGING All the arthropods shown here have an exoskeleton. The cicada's new exoskeleton (above) has already formed beneath the old one.

Centipede

Scorpion

Tick

CLASSIFYING INSECTS

All insects have certain characteristics in common, the most obvious of these being a body divided into three parts and usually three pairs of jointed legs. But with more than 1 million species of insect identified by scientists, and the possibility that there might be 30 million in total, a method for identifying and classifying species is essential.

Butterflies and moths (Lepidoptera)

TAXONOMIC SYSTEM

Zoologists classify animals on the basis of structure. Animals with features in common are placed together in a group. Those with other characteristics are placed in other groups. These groups are divided and divided again, until there is a taxonomic group with many characteristics in common.

All class Insects are classified under the Phylum Arthropoda, Class Insecta. Insects have bodies that are usually divided into three parts: the head, the thorax, and

CLASSIFYING CHARACTERISTICS

This green scarab beetle belongs to the largest order of insects, the Coleoptera, which has more than 350,000 species. All species in this order have armored bodies and hardened wing cases, called elytra. Scarabs belong to the Family Scarabaeidae. Scientists assign a unique name to each species and place it within this structure.

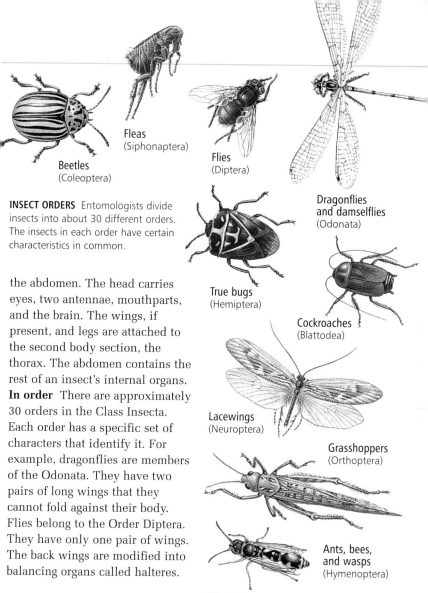

Beetles
(Coleoptera)

Fleas
(Siphonaptera)

Flies
(Diptera)

Dragonflies
and damselflies
(Odonata)

INSECT ORDERS Entomologists divide insects into about 30 different orders. The insects in each order have certain characteristics in common.

True bugs
(Hemiptera)

Cockroaches
(Blattodea)

Lacewings
(Neuroptera)

Grasshoppers
(Orthoptera)

Ants, bees,
and wasps
(Hymenoptera)

the abdomen. The head carries eyes, two antennae, mouthparts, and the brain. The wings, if present, and legs are attached to the second body section, the thorax. The abdomen contains the rest of an insect's internal organs.

In order There are approximately 30 orders in the Class Insecta. Each order has a specific set of characters that identify it. For example, dragonflies are members of the Odonata. They have two pairs of long wings that they cannot fold against their body. Flies belong to the Order Diptera. They have only one pair of wings. The back wings are modified into balancing organs called halteres.

INSECT COVER STORY

Insects and their relatives have adapted to living on Earth more successfully than any other type of animal. In fact, today, they make up more than half of all the species on Earth. The basic insect body plan has become modified through the process of evolution, resulting in a group of animals superbly adapted to their habitats.

DRESS FOR SUCCESS

Insects have many features that have contributed to their phenomenal success. Their exoskeleton helps to protect them from environmental stresses and from predation. Many have developed protective coloration, mimicry, and defensive chemicals to deter predators. Their small size and energy-efficient physiology have helped them survive in virtually every habitat. Adaptable wings, legs, and mouthparts have allowed them to exploit many food sources. An advanced sensory system allows most insects to sense danger, send signals to mates, find prey, and to survive in hot or dry habitats.

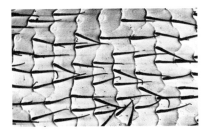

HAIR SENSE An ant's leg is covered with tiny, sensitive hairs that send information about motion, temperature, and chemicals to the insect's brain.

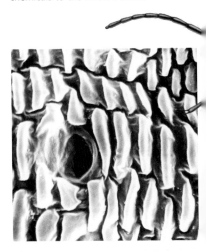

HOLE STORY This electron micrograph shows a spiracle, the opening to an insect's respiratory system. Rows of spiracles are on the thorax or abdomen.

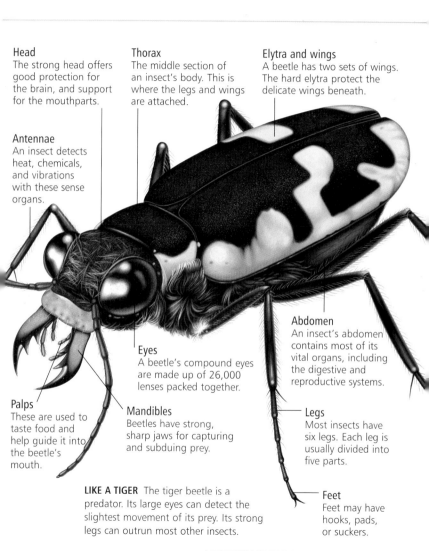

Head
The strong head offers good protection for the brain, and support for the mouthparts.

Thorax
The middle section of an insect's body. This is where the legs and wings are attached.

Elytra and wings
A beetle has two sets of wings. The hard elytra protect the delicate wings beneath.

Antennae
An insect detects heat, chemicals, and vibrations with these sense organs.

Abdomen
An insect's abdomen contains most of its vital organs, including the digestive and reproductive systems.

Eyes
A beetle's compound eyes are made up of 26,000 lenses packed together.

Palps
These are used to taste food and help guide it into the beetle's mouth.

Mandibles
Beetles have strong, sharp jaws for capturing and subduing prey.

Legs
Most insects have six legs. Each leg is usually divided into five parts.

Feet
Feet may have hooks, pads, or suckers.

LIKE A TIGER The tiger beetle is a predator. Its large eyes can detect the slightest movement of its prey. Its strong legs can outrun most other insects.

Inside an Insect

■ Inside an insect's body, many different systems are at work. Like most animals, insects eat, breathe, move, and reproduce. Blood, usually yellow or green in color, carries nutrients to the body parts and removes wastes, and is pumped by a long, thin heart that stretches through the body.

Breathe in Insects have no lungs. Instead, they get oxygen through openings along the sides of their bodies, called spiracles. Spiracles are connected to tracheae, which branch into smaller tubes. These carry oxygen to every part of the insect. Each spiracle can open or shut, depending on how much oxygen is required.

Nerve center All bodily functions are controlled by the large brain, which is connected to all nerves by a long nerve cord. Clusters of nerve cells along the nerve cord, called ganglia, collect signals from the sense organs and carry messages from one part of the body to another.

Burning energy To keep all these systems running, an insect needs energy from food. In the case of this wasp (right), the food is mixed with saliva in the mouth. It passes down the throat to the crop, where it is broken down by more saliva. It then passes to the stomach, where special enzymes churn up the food further, making it ready for the insect to use.

DOWN THE TUBE Some water-dwelling insects, such as this water scorpion, breathe oxygen at the surface through a tiny tube attached to their abdomen.

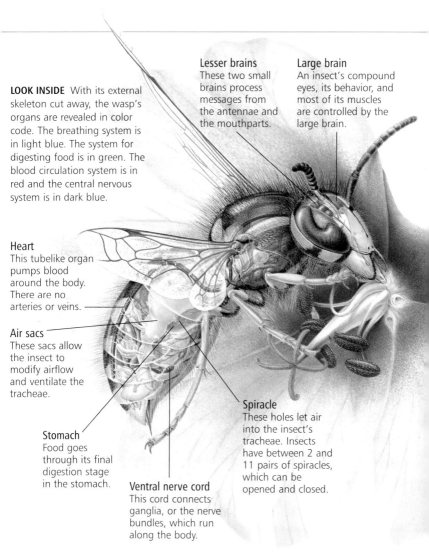

LOOK INSIDE With its external skeleton cut away, the wasp's organs are revealed in color code. The breathing system is in light blue. The system for digesting food is in green. The blood circulation system is in red and the central nervous system is in dark blue.

Lesser brains
These two small brains process messages from the antennae and the mouthparts.

Large brain
An insect's compound eyes, its behavior, and most of its muscles are controlled by the large brain.

Heart
This tubelike organ pumps blood around the body. There are no arteries or veins.

Air sacs
These sacs allow the insect to modify airflow and ventilate the tracheae.

Stomach
Food goes through its final digestion stage in the stomach.

Ventral nerve cord
This cord connects ganglia, or the nerve bundles, which run along the body.

Spiracle
These holes let air into the insect's tracheae. Insects have between 2 and 11 pairs of spiracles, which can be opened and closed.

CLASSIFYING ARACHNIDS

Like insects, spiders and their relatives are arthropods. They have jointed legs and a hard exoskeleton, or carapace.

TWO-PART BODIES

Spiders and their allies are in the Class Arachnida, which includes scorpions, mites, and ticks. They differ from insects in having two rather than three body segments and four pairs of jointed legs.

A diverse group Arachnids are a diverse group of eight orders. They vary in size from tiny mites, smaller than a pinhead, to tarantulas the size of a plate.

The sting Spiders have powerful jaws equipped with fangs that can deliver venom to paralyze prey.

Scientists differentiate spiders into two groups, according to the way they move their fangs to stab prey (see opposite).

Top and tail Scorpions differ from spiders in having an abdomen that is divided into 12 segments. The last five segments make up the upturned tail, or telson, which has a poisonous stinger on its tip.

Mites and ticks have an unsegmented abdomen. Most species are less than 1/32 inch (1 mm) long. Both eat liquid food with their piercing mouthparts.

MITE AND POWER Mites (above) appear to have one body part, but they have two. Scorpions (left) have a segmented abdomen, eight legs, pedipalps, and a venomous tail stinger.

SPURRED ON The shape is unusual, but this *Micrathena* spider still displays the characteristics common to the order Aranea—spiders.

FANGS DIVIDE Spiders are classified into two main types by the way they use their fangs. Mygalomorph fangs hinge downwards and araneomorph fangs hinge together and sideways.

Mygalomorph

Araneomorph

ARACHNID ANATOMY

Arachnids vary greatly in appearance, but the major groups have characteristics that are relatively easy to identify.

HEAD AND LEGS

Arachnid bodies are divided into two parts: a fused head and thorax, called a cephalothorax or prosoma, and an abdomen, or opisthosoma. All arachnids have eight walking legs and never have antennae or wings. Arachnids have a pair of chelicerae, which in the case of spiders, have fangs attached. Pedipalps are modified legs that carry out many functions, including the manipulation of food and the capturing of prey. In scorpions, the pedipalps are

SILK SPINNERS Most spiders have three or four pairs of spinnerets. These deliver the liquid silk to the outside. As the spider tugs on it with its legs, the silk hardens.

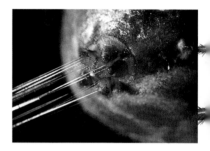

enlarged and bear a large, pincer-like claw.

Eyes have it Spiders have a group of six to twelve simple eyes. One pair of eyes forms the image, while the surrounding eyes detect movement. Most species have poor vision and rely on sensing movement through body hairs. They also have slits in their exoskeleton that are sensitive to vibrations.

FATAL FANGS A spider's venom is stored in glands at the base of its fangs. When the spider bites, venom flows through a small hole at the tip of the fang.

Eye
Most spiders have eight simple eyes in two rows. Some have excellent vision; others have no eyes at all.

Abdomen
This soft body part contains the lungs and the silk-making glands, and other vital organs.

Chelicera
The fangs are attached to the chelicerae, or jaws.

Claw
Many spiders have tiny claws and hairs on their legs that help them grip their webs.

Cephalothorax
The head and the thorax are fused together in arachnids. The jaws and the legs are attached here.

Leg
All spiders have eight jointed legs. They are covered in hairs that are extremely sensitive to movement.

Pedipalp
These modified legs help to sense and manipulate food. Males also use them to transfer sperm during mating.

WELCOME WEBS Not all spiders are dangerous to humans. This marbled orb weaver is a natural pest controller, eating more than 350 flies and wasps in its lifetime.

Inside a Spider

■ A spider's internal body systems are similar to those of other arachnids and insects. The cephalothorax houses the sensory organs, poison glands, sucking stomach, and the brain. The remainder of its vital organs— heart, lung, digestive gland, reproductive organs, and silk gland—are found in the abdomen.

INSIDE OUT
A spider's nervous system consists of a brain—the main control center—and a series of nerve bundles, or ganglia.
Life blood Spiders have a long, tubular heart that pumps nutrient-rich blood to its organs.
Book to breathe Most spiders obtain oxygen through a book lung, so named because it contains many flat sheets like a book. These sheets increase the surface area of the lung.
Liquid lunch Spiders must partially digest their food before they eat it. Most inject their prey with paralyzing venom and digestive enzymes to dissolve the victim's tissues.

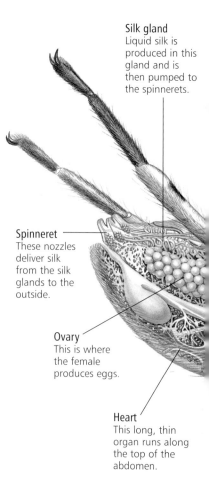

Silk gland
Liquid silk is produced in this gland and is then pumped to the spinnerets.

Spinneret
These nozzles deliver silk from the silk glands to the outside.

Ovary
This is where the female produces eggs.

Heart
This long, thin organ runs along the top of the abdomen.

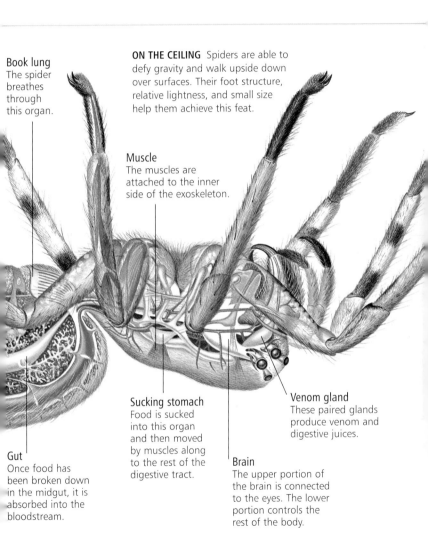

Book lung
The spider breathes through this organ.

ON THE CEILING Spiders are able to defy gravity and walk upside down over surfaces. Their foot structure, relative lightness, and small size help them achieve this feat.

Muscle
The muscles are attached to the inner side of the exoskeleton.

Sucking stomach
Food is sucked into this organ and then moved by muscles along to the rest of the digestive tract.

Venom gland
These paired glands produce venom and digestive juices.

Gut
Once food has been broken down in the midgut, it is absorbed into the bloodstream.

Brain
The upper portion of the brain is connected to the eyes. The lower portion controls the rest of the body.

The Life of Insects and Spiders

INSECTS, SPIDERS, AND THEIR RELATIVES have adapted to life
on Earth more successfully than any other animal group.
Their vast distribution and thriving success are due largely
to their small size, their sophisticated sensory systems,
and their many and varied survival strategies.
As a result, these creatures live in a bewildering array
of environments, from the base of a mammal's eyelash
to the frozen Arctic tundra.

HOMES AND HABITATS

Insects and spiders are found almost everywhere on Earth, from freezing mountain peaks to dry, inhospitable deserts. Some live in highly urbanized areas and others thrive living on the bodies of other animals. Certain alpine species can survive at temperatures below -40°F (-40°C), while some desert insects are able to withstand temperatures in excess of 104°F (40°C). Many insects cope with the extreme temperatures by becoming dormant, re-emerging when

HIDDEN JEWELS Flower mantids live in most tropical habitats around the world. Their superb camouflage allows them to pounce on unsuspecting insect prey.

conditions have normalized. Survival strategies such as this, teamed with their small size, their protective casing, and speedy reproductive methods, have afforded insects the largest range of all animal species.

HABITAT DIVERSITY

Insect diversity is low in polar regions, but numbers may be great, especially in summer. The variety and number of species are greater near the equator, especially in tropical rainforests.

Vital role Insects and spiders play an essential role in the maintenance of the Earth's food chains and ecosystems. They pollinate flowers and help to recycle and return nutrients to the soil by eating decomposing plant and animal material. Protecting insect habitat from destruction is of paramount importance if these ecosystems are to be maintained.

FRAGILE SILVER This silver scarab lives in the cloud forests of Costa Rica. These forests are at risk from deforestation.

Deserts and Grasslands

■ There are many contrasts between arid deserts and vast areas of swaying grassland, but insect and spider species flourish in these dry environments.

HEAT HAZE

Desert-dwellers live with little moisture and in extremes of temperature. Most species avoid the day's heat by being active in the cooler dawn or dusk. Giant desert scorpions and tarantulas venture out at this time to search for mates and food. Ants seem to thrive in temperatures that would be fatal to other species. After rainfall, many desert plants produce masses of flowers, which provide an abundance of food for insects, as well as pollination opportunities for the plant.

Tall grass Tropical and temperate grasslands provide rich habitats for many species, especially ants and termites. Moths, hover flies, and bees feed on the flowering plants, grasshoppers chew seeds, and spiders spin webs between the grass stalks to capture prey.

IN THE GROOVE

This darkling beetle lives in Africa's Namib Desert. The only regular moisture available in this dry habitat is the fog that comes rolling in from the coast. In order to utilize this resource, the beetle points its abdomen into the wind and collects the moisture that condenses on its body. The water droplets pool in a groove on the beetle's body and trickle down to its mouth.

HOT SPOTS To survive the dry desert environment, honey ants (above) store nectar and water in their abdomens. Many scorpion species (right) have adapted to the desert extremes.

Woodlands and Rainforests

■ The variety and abundance of insects and spiders is at its pinnacle in the Earth's tropical rainforests. Arthropods thrive in the ideal conditions of a constant temperature and high humidity. There is also huge fauna diversity in temperate woodlands, where many micro-habitats—including soil, leaf-litter, broad leaves, and rotting wood—are available to insects and spiders.

HOTHOUSE

The fertile, shaded environment of the rainforest is home to millions of arthropods, many of which are yet to be described by scientists. The canopy gives shelter from temperature

SKY GARDEN It is estimated that more than half of all the world's arthropod species live in moist, tropical rainforest. Species living high in the canopy remain for the most part unstudied.

fluctuations, and flowers and foliage provide year-round food supplies for adults and larvae. Mantids, beetles, ants, butterflies, and spiders use camouflage to avoid being eaten. Often, the most bizarre examples of camouflage are found in rainforests. Some species mimic unpalatable animals to discourage predators. **Wooded wonderland** Temperate old-growth forests have extremely fertile soil because of the constant

SIPPING NECTAR Swallowtail butterflies are found worldwide, especially in warmer woodlands and rainforests, where flowering plants are abundant.

vegetation decay. The thick layer of leaf litter and lush understory of shrubs houses a myriad of arthropod species. Ants, termites, beetles, scorpions, and spiders all thrive in these conditions, where there are plenty of small invertebrates available as food.

Underwater and Underground

■ Many insects and spiders have aquatic or fossorial (underground) habits. They display unique specializations to ensure survival in these environments.

WATER WORLD

Aquatic insects are streamlined to help them move swiftly through water to escape predators and find food.

Holding breath Whirligig beetles live on pond surfaces. They have divided compound eyes that can see above and below water at the same time. Water boatmen and diving beetles trap air under their wing cases as oxygen reserves. The European water spider constructs a diving bell out of silk, filling it with air bubbles it drags from the surface.

The seashore offers another niche for insects, including beetles and flies that feed on decaying seaweed.

GONE TO GROUND

Underground or cave-dwelling insects must adapt to low light or total darkness. Many have eyes reduced to light-sensitive patches. Some are wingless, while others have extremely long antennae for detecting prey in low light.

THE GOOD OIL

Some insects live in extremely harsh habitats and conditions. The petroleum fly lives in puddles of crude oil. It feeds on other insects that fall into the oil and get stuck.

WATER SENSE Whirligigs locate food by creating ripples and sensing how they bounce back.

GILL FANS This damselfly nymph can extract oxygen from the water through its fanlike gills.

LITTLE DIGGER The nocturnal Jerusalem cricket lives its life mostly underground. It has strong legs for digging but unlike other crickets, it is wingless.

POND LIFE The bodies of aquatic insects are often streamlined to help them glide through water. Water boatmen paddle through the water with oarlike legs. Water striders use surface tension to skate across the water's surface.

Animal Hosts

■ Parasitic arthropods, such as ticks, mites, and lice, feed on the living tissue or blood of a host animal. Although most will not kill the host, they cause blood loss and may carry diseases.

GIANT LEAP A flea springs from host to host using specialized muscles in its thorax. It can jump up to 100 times its own height.

LIVING TOGETHER
Parasitic arthropods have mouthparts or appendages specially adapted for feeding on their host's tissues. Some also have flattened bodies for burrowing through skin layers.

Fleas have heat-sensitive antennae to sense the body heat of a passing mammal, or the presence of carbon dioxide exhaled by the potential host.

FULL BLOWN After two days of sucking blood, a female tick expands up to 200 times its own weight.

Cling-ons Human head and body lice have legs equipped with strong claws for gripping. The head louse lives its entire life in hair, gluing its eggs, called nits, to the base of hair shafts. The micro-organism that causes typhus is carried by body lice and is transmitted to the host through contact. Some lice live on sea mammals. These lice can survive long periods in salt water, an unusual feat for insects.

Skin deep Scabies mites feed on the skin and hair of mammals, including humans. They burrow into the epidermis, leaving visible tunnels in the skin's surface. The host's scratching often results in a secondary infection. Mites penetrate the exoskeleton of many insects, usually at the body joints, where the cuticle is thinnest.

BEDBUG BITE Bedbugs use their piercing mouthparts to feed on human blood. They are active at night, but hide away in bedding and clothes during the day. They find their host by sensing body heat.

TICK OFF Ticks often feed in clusters on their hosts, using chelicerae adapted for piercing and sucking. They are significant carriers of human and animal disease.

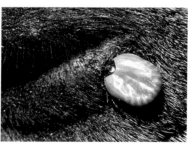

FORM AND FUNCTION

The basic insect and arachnid body plans have been modified in a variety of ways through the process of evolution. These specializations mean insects and spiders increase their chances of survival and pass this success to their future progeny.

WINGS AND THINGS

Because insects are small they can inhabit a wide range of micro-habitats—for example, a decaying log may be home to hundreds of different species. Fast reproductive rates allow a high rate of evolution and adaptation to environmental conditions. As a result, insect adaptations are many and varied.
Good sense An insect's antennae can sense sound and vibration, but can also detect chemical messages from a potential mate or pass on information about food.
Leg up Insect legs have been modified for digging, swimming, jumping, and even hearing. An insect's wings are used for flight, but they may also have a protective function. Mouthparts are modified to bite, slice, or suck nectar or blood. An insect's coloration can be used for camouflage, to attract a mate, or confuse a potential predator.
Spider forms Although the arachnid body plan displays greater uniformity, spiders in particular have developed sensory specializations associated with hunting and web-spinning. The development of cryptic coloration and mimicry has served not only to protect spiders from predators, but has also helped disguise them from their victims.

STEALTH AND SPEED The front legs of a praying mantis (above) are modified for catching prey. Wasps (right) are superbly adapted as flying predators.

Focus on Flight

■ Insects were the first animals to fly. It is the key to their immense success and incredible diversity. Today, they are still the most numerous fliers in the animal world. Flying allows insects to escape from danger, and find new habitats. It also makes it easier for them to find mates and establish new colonies. One of flight's most important benefits is that insects can reach and exploit a huge variety of food sources.

FLYING SUCCESS

Insects have been flying for more than 300 million years, since wings evolved from the gills on aquatic nymphs. The first fliers probably did little more than glide, but as wing design improved through the process of evolution, flying became more reliable and sophisticated. The earliest fliers were not able to fold their wings back alongside their bodies, but as this ability developed, the radiation and success of insects began in earnest. The only insects today unable to fold their wings are the dragonflies and mayflies.

Places to go Modern insects vary greatly in the distances they fly. Some insects manage only a few yards, while others embark on journeys of thousands of miles.

WING BEATS All the insects shown below are strong fliers. They achieve this through beating their wings at vastly different speeds.

Dragonfly
35 beats/sec

Housefly
170 beats/sec

Honeybee
130 beats/sec

Butterfly
10 beats/sec

Mosquito
600 beats/sec

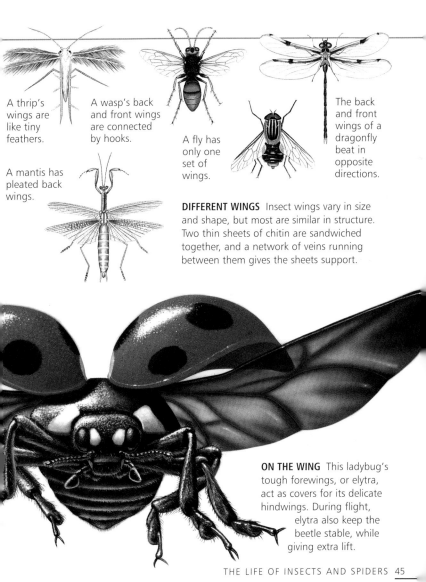

A thrip's wings are like tiny feathers.

A wasp's back and front wings are connected by hooks.

A fly has only one set of wings.

The back and front wings of a dragonfly beat in opposite directions.

A mantis has pleated back wings.

DIFFERENT WINGS Insect wings vary in size and shape, but most are similar in structure. Two thin sheets of chitin are sandwiched together, and a network of veins running between them gives the sheets support.

ON THE WING This ladybug's tough forewings, or elytra, act as covers for its delicate hindwings. During flight, elytra also keep the beetle stable, while giving extra lift.

Taking to the Air

■ Although most insects have wings, not all are accomplished fliers. Many species, such as scorpion flies, need to launch themselves from a high point to gain enough lift for them to take off. By contrast, the two-winged flies are strong and fast fliers, displaying impressive maneuverability in the air.

LIFT-OFF POWER

An insect's wings are powered by strong muscles in the thorax. Unlike birds and bats, the flight muscles of insects are not directly attached to the wings. Instead, the muscles change the shape of the thorax and the wings move in response. Each wing is connected to the thorax by a tiny plate or joint called a sclerite. This joint allows the wing to move up or down, backward or forward, giving it extra control in the air.

More than a beat To fly, an insect must tilt its wings and beat them. This pushes air backward, which gives the insect thrust. When the wings are at the top of the upstroke, their front edges are

WIND POWER

Some insects, such as thrips (below) and some aphids, are too small and slow to get very far under their own wing power. Instead, they rely on the power of wind currents to blow them from one place to another.

FAST FLIGHT Dragonflies are the fastest fliers in the insect world. During flight, they can reach speeds of more than 31 miles (50 km) per hour.

raised. As the downstroke begins, the front edges start to dip. The greater the angle of the edges, the stronger the thrust, and the faster the insect travels.

WING WATCHING

Flying insects have two pairs of wings attached to their thorax. Wings are made from chitin, the same hard material that covers the rest of the body. Butterflies and dragonflies use both pairs of wings to fly. In some insects, wings are covered by minute hairs. In butterflies and moths, the wings are made up of tiny, overlapping scales, each reflecting light to produce the brilliant colors. In some species, such as honeybees, the larger forewings are joined to the hindwings by a row of hooks, so that the two pairs beat in unison.

Flying aces Flies are the aviation experts of the insect world. Unlike almost all other flying insects, they have only a single pair of wings, which gives them great speed and agility in the air. Their hindwings have been modified into small, club-like balancing organs called halteres.

FLIGHT INSTRUMENTS The crane fly's halteres vibrate at high speeds during flight to keep its body balanced and level. Modern ships use a similar technique to stabilize them during a storm.

These organs monitor the insect's movements while it is in the air. Hover flies display such precision in flight that they can slow down, change direction suddenly, hover in the same spot, and even fly backwards. Houseflies flip themselves over in midair, ready to land upside down on a ceiling.

Flight check Unlike warm-blooded birds and bats, insects must warm up their flight muscles before they become airborne. To achieve this, they vibrate their wings for a time before a flight or they simply bask in the sun until the correct muscle temperature is reached.

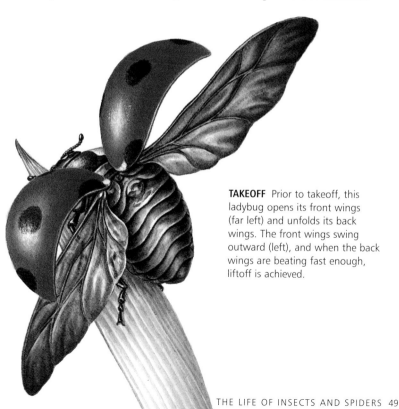

TAKEOFF Prior to takeoff, this ladybug opens its front wings (far left) and unfolds its back wings. The front wings swing outward (left), and when the back wings are beating fast enough, liftoff is achieved.

SENSING SURROUNDINGS

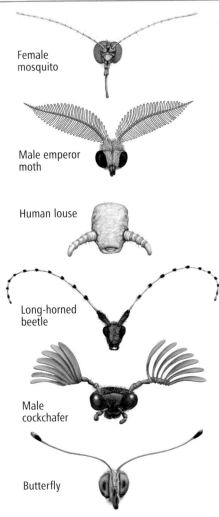

Female mosquito

Male emperor moth

Human louse

Long-horned beetle

Male cockchafer

Butterfly

Insects have five main senses—sight, smell, touch, taste, and hearing—which they use to monitor their surroundings, find a mate, and avoid predators. Each insect type specializes in using some senses more than others.

TUNING IN

Much of the information an insect receives is filtered through its antennae, which enable it to smell, touch, and hear. The shape of antennae varies greatly among insects and sometimes even between males and females of the same species (see left).

Sight Most insects have compound eyes, which are made of many smaller eyes, called eyelets, packed tightly together. Some eyes may have as many as 56,000 lenses, each recording a different view. Many insects also have simple eyes on the top of their heads, called ocelli, to help with flight and light detection.

Good taste Insects taste food using sense organs clustered around the mouth, the most important being the palps.

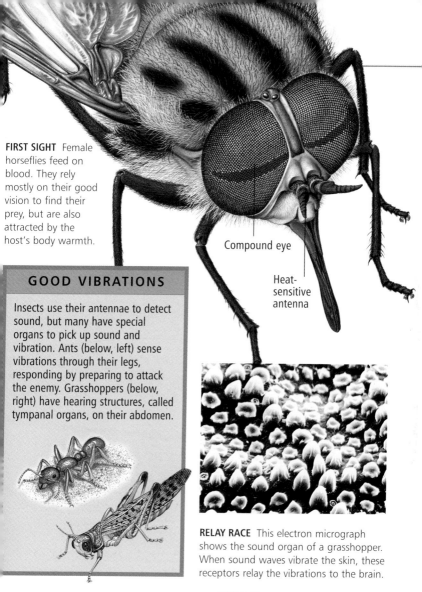

FIRST SIGHT Female horseflies feed on blood. They rely mostly on their good vision to find their prey, but are also attracted by the host's body warmth.

Compound eye

Heat-sensitive antenna

GOOD VIBRATIONS

Insects use their antennae to detect sound, but many have special organs to pick up sound and vibration. Ants (below, left) sense vibrations through their legs, responding by preparing to attack the enemy. Grasshoppers (below, right) have hearing structures, called tympanal organs, on their abdomen.

RELAY RACE This electron micrograph shows the sound organ of a grasshopper. When sound waves vibrate the skin, these receptors relay the vibrations to the brain.

SPIDER SENSE

All spiders are predators. Most species trap their food in silken webs, but many actively hunt for food or wait in ambush for it. These different methods require specialized sensory organs. Because most spiders are solitary, they must also rely on their senses to detect the signals that will guide them to a mate.

EYES ON MOVEMENT

A spider sees the world through a group of eyes along the front of its cephalothorax. One pair of eyes forms images, while the ancillary eyes detect movement. Although hunting spiders, such as wolf and jumping spiders, have excellent vision, spiders for the most part have poor eyesight.

NET CAPTURE A spider senses struggling prey ensnared in its web using slits in its exoskeleton that can detect vibration.

Spider sensitivity Because many spiders have poor vision, they rely instead on sensitive body hairs to convey information about prey. Each hair is anchored in a tiny pit surrounded by nerve endings. A vibration from any direction will move the hair. Some spiders also have tiny slits in their exoskeletons that are sensitive to vibrations. Web-spinning spiders use these sense organs to detect if prey is trapped in their web.

Fine sensory hairs are abundant on the pedipalps and legs of arachnids. These are used for smelling and tasting.

LEGS AND EYES Sensitive hairs on spiders' legs (left) detect prey caught in their web. The ogre-faced spider's large eyes (right) see in near total darkness. Crab spiders (right) rely on vibration sensors, only seeing with their eyes as prey approaches.

Ogre-faced spider
Night vision

Crab spider
Sit and wait

Insect and Spider Behavior

Despite their relatively small brain size, insects,
spiders, and their relatives display remarkably sophisticated
behavior. Most groups lead solitary lives, but others—
the social insects—are characterized by cooperation
and division of labor within their huge colonies.
This chapter explores the complex and often extraordinary
behavior of insects and spiders: how they communicate,
find food, avoid predators, and how they reproduce to
ensure the future of their species.

STAYING IN TOUCH

Insects have sophisticated sensory systems for such small creatures. They are able to respond to a range of physical, chemical, and visual stimuli. Many can sense infra-red radiation or ultraviolet light, magnetic fields, or humidity fluctuations. Insects communicate with one another using sight, sound, touch, and taste—and even light. Many have bright colors or patterns to identify themselves to others. Most butterflies and dragonflies recognize each other's markings, with males often being the most colorful partners.

Light show Fireflies and other organisms can produce cold light—called bioluminescence—by mixing chemicals together in the body. Males and females

NIGHT LIGHTS This female firefly communicates by flashing a code on her glowing abdomen to males performing a special dance in the sky above her.

flash coded signals to one another through the darkness.

Sounding off For crickets, cicadas, and some smaller insects, sound provides a way to contact a mate. Unlike sight, sound works during the day and night, and allows an insect to stay hidden while it broadcasts its call.

Touch and taste Insects often use touch and taste to communicate, but they can also make contact by smell. Some of their scents, or pheromones, waft considerable distances through the air. Others mark the ground with scent to show where they have been.

DIFFERENT WAYS

Insects employ many other ways of communicating. Lacewings and treehoppers stamp messages on the branches they sit on. Aquatic insects such as water striders and backswimmers sense vibrations in the water with their feet.

SMELL CHECK Some insects use chemicals called pheromones to communicate. Red ants touch with their antennae to check smells and see if they are from the same nest. Invaders are quickly expelled.

DISTANT CALLS

The Y-shaped burrow of the male mole cricket helps to amplify his call. He produces his sound by scraping his left front wing against his right—much like a fingernail against a comb. In fact, it is one of the loudest calls in the insect world, and in still air it can be heard more than half a mile (800 m) away.

Front legs used for digging

Spider Communication

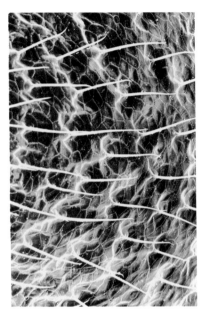

FEEL THE BREEZE The sensory hairs on a spider's body are crucial for detecting stimuli from the surroundings and for communicating with its own species.

As solitary predators, most spiders communicate only when they come together to mate. Communication strategies depend largely on the sensory capabilities of the species; those with good eyesight use visual signals and those with poor eyesight use touch and vibration. Some web-spinning spiders prefer to use scent messages, coating their silk with pheromones.

COURTSHIP DISPLAYS

Most spiders live alone and treat approaches by others as a threat. Males often have elaborate courtship displays that are designed to signal their intentions to mate with a female, therefore avoiding attack, and possible death, by the female.

Dance recital Spiders with good eyesight usually display to females by waving their legs or pedipalps in a special, sometimes

MORSE CODE A male spider sends signals to a potential mate by tapping a specific code on her web as he approaches. In this way, he avoids being attacked.

MATING DANCE A male jumping spider signals a female by waving his front legs in the air and maneuvering his body to display his colors and patterns. The female recognizes him as one of her species and a potential mate. He moves closer, stroking her and then mating with her.

intricate sequence. Once recognized as one of her own species and not a rival, the female will allow the male to approach and mate with her.

Web song Male web-spinning spiders avoid being eaten when courting a female by signaling to her using a species-specific code. He tugs on the female's web in a particular sequence as he tentatively moves toward her. If the approach is accepted, the pair will mate.

Grating sounds Some male spiders have stridulating organs that they use to produce a high-pitched grating sound while they are in the female's web. In one species, the male has minute bristles on his legs that are rubbed on the surface of his book lung to produce a vibration.

Ripple soles Male nursery-web spiders live on the water's edge. They send ripple messages across the water when courting. Sensory slit organs on the female's feet detect the ripples on the surface.

FROM EGG TO ADULT

Virtually all insects start out life as eggs. Adults come together to mate and females lay fertilized eggs that eventually develop into adults. One notable exception to this sequence is female aphids, which may produce thousands of offspring by parthenogenesis, a process whereby eggs develop without fertilization. In the insect world, the development of an egg into an adult requires periods of growth and the shedding of the exoskeleton to increase size. Arachnids molt throughout their lives, and the young look like small versions of the adults.

TRANSFORMATIONS

With the exception of silverfish and bristletails, all insects change their appearance on their journey to adulthood. For dragonflies, damselflies, grasshoppers, termites, mantids, and cockroaches, this process is a gradual one. It is usually termed "incomplete" metamorphosis. In more advanced insects, the immature stage, called a larva, looks completely different from the adult. Instead of many gradual changes, the larva reorganizes its immature tissues during pupation and makes one dramatic transformation to adulthood. This is called "complete" metamorphosis. The larvae focus on feeding and growth, and the adults complete the lifecycle with reproduction and dispersal.

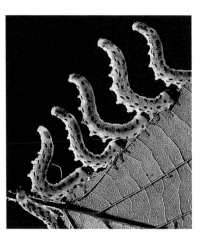

BODY CHANGES Sawfly larvae (left) eat voraciously before they transform into adults. A dragonfly (right) emerges from its final nymphal skin as a winged adult.

Passing on the Genes

■ In most arthropod species, males and females come together to mate before the female lays her eggs. Mating may occur when individuals are gathered together at a food or water source. For other species, sophisticated sensory and physical signals are used to court a mate, including the use of odors, sounds, or displays. Sometimes males fight with rivals for the right to mate.

NEW GENERATION

Males deliver their sperm to females in a packet called a spermatophore. This packet is either deposited into the female's genital pore or is picked up by the female herself. Females often store sperm in special organs

GETTING TOGETHER Sperm transfer to a female may take only a few minutes, but some males clasp the female to ensure she does not mate with other males.

inside the body for use when conditions are optimal. Male spiders transfer sperm to their pedipalps using a specially woven sperm web. The palps draw up drops of sperm when they are dipped into the web and this is then transferred to the female's genital opening.

Bearing gifts Copulation may last from a few seconds to many hours. In some species, mating is preceded by an elaborate courtship ritual or by the presentation of food offerings from the male to his mate.

RULE OF CLAW Male hercules beetles use their enlarged mandibles to fight for the right to mate with a female.

Eggs

Horsefly eggs

Eucalyptus tip bug eggs

■ Almost all insects and arachnids lay eggs. The eggs develop outside the female's body and are usually laid near a suitable food source. Many plant-eating species must lay their eggs on plants that are suitable for their hatched larvae.

COMPLETE PACKAGE
A female sometimes lays single eggs, but more often eggs are laid in clusters of hundreds or even thousands. During her lifetime, a queen termite can lay more than 10 million eggs.

Female insects lay eggs through a specialized tube on their abdomen called the ovipositor. Some eggs hatch soon after being laid, but others stay inactive during months of cold or dry weather, during which all the adults may die. Some eggs hatch inside the mother's body, with live young emerging from the genital pore.

Young and alone Most females make no attempt to care for their eggs. However, the giant water bug and some shield bugs will protect their young from danger.

MOTHER LOVE In what is unusual behavior in insects, the female shield bug protects her eggs and young. She will try to scare predators away if they threaten.

BORING DETAILS The female ichneumon wasp (right) drills into wood with her modified ovipositor. She stings the larva of a wood wasp and deposits her eggs into it. When the eggs hatch, they will feed on the host.

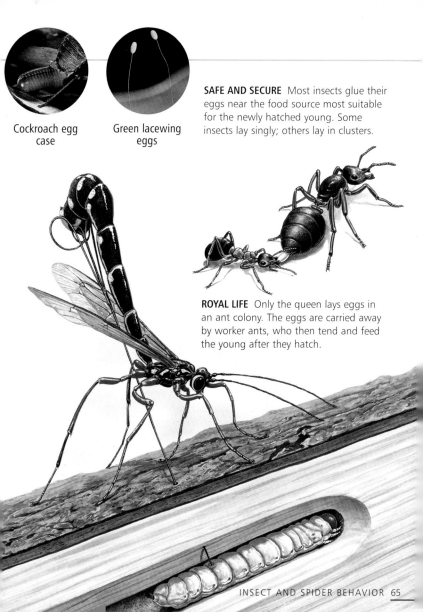

Cockroach egg
case

Green lacewing
eggs

SAFE AND SECURE Most insects glue their eggs near the food source most suitable for the newly hatched young. Some insects lay singly; others lay in clusters.

ROYAL LIFE Only the queen lays eggs in an ant colony. The eggs are carried away by worker ants, who then tend and feed the young after they hatch.

Nests and Shelters

■ Insects are among the most experienced of nature's builders. They construct many different structures to house and protect their families.

BUILDING PROJECTS

Some insects work alone to build simple shelters just for themselves or for their young. Others—the termites, ants, social bees, and wasps—work in family groups. Their nests are far more ambitious, and many are large enough to house millions of individuals. Social insects use a range of building materials, from leaves and dead plants to wood fibers, mud, and wax. They chew up the material to form a paste and spread the paste where it is needed. Termite mounds range in size from tiny nests to enormous above- and below-ground structures (see opposite). Weaver ants make nests by pulling together leaves and gluing them with a sticky fluid secreted by their larvae. Honeybees use wax secretions to construct hives of hexagonal cells. These intricate building tasks are all guided by instinctual behavior.

SPIDER NESTS

Spiders produce silk cocoons to protect their developing young. In some cases, the sacs are placed in a safe location and then deserted. Some species guard their eggs and young, and may even carry them on their bodies. The water spider places her silk-cocooned eggs in the top of her submerged home.

IN THE POT The female potter wasp places a caterpillar in a mud nest, lays an egg, and seals the pot. After the grub hatches, it eats the caterpillar.

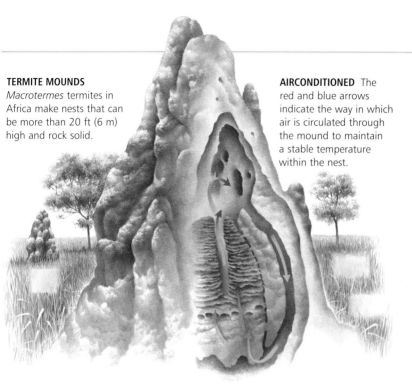

TERMITE MOUNDS
Macrotermes termites in Africa make nests that can be more than 20 ft (6 m) high and rock solid.

AIRCONDITIONED The red and blue arrows indicate the way in which air is circulated through the mound to maintain a stable temperature within the nest.

1 The queen starts the nest by building a hanging cup from chewed wood fibers.

2 She makes cells inside the cup in which she lays her eggs.

3 The eggs hatch into worker wasps, which work to expand the nest.

COMMUNAL LIVING When the nest of the common wasp is completed, it may contain more than 10,000 cells.

Journey to Adulthood

■ Insects such as earwigs, dragonflies, grasshoppers, true bugs, and mantids undergo an incomplete metamorphosis. This process involves the gradual transformation of a larva into an adult through a succession of molts and physical changes. The immature stages of this process are called nymphs. Nymphs look similar to the adult, but they are wingless, different in color, and lack any reproductive structures. Wings grow gradually on the outside of a nymph's body. During the final molt, the nymph emerges from its old exoskeleton as an adult with functional wings.

NYMPH TO ADULT Dragonfly nymphs spend up to five years developing underwater before climbing up a plant stem, molting their skin for the last time, and emerging as adults, able to fly.

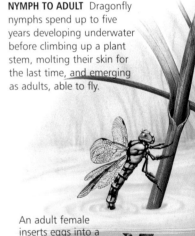

An adult female inserts eggs into a water plant.

Each tiny nymph chews its way out of its egg case.

MAYFLY LIFE

A female mayfly spends up to three years as a nymph, but will live for just one day as an adult. She cannot eat or drink, because she has no mouthparts. Her only purpose is to mate with a male and lay eggs to ensure the next generation.

Some cicada species take up to 17 years to mature underground. Millions of adults emerge together. The cicadas mate and lay eggs and the cycle is repeated. Nymphs often live in similar habitats and feed on similar food to the adult insect. Damselfly and dragonfly nymphs are less like the adult they transform into. They live in ponds and use gills on their tail to take in oxygen.

The nymph bursts its old skin and emerges as an adult.

A male and female mate.

The nymph climbs out of the water.

The nymph catches tadpoles and worms.

Life Changes

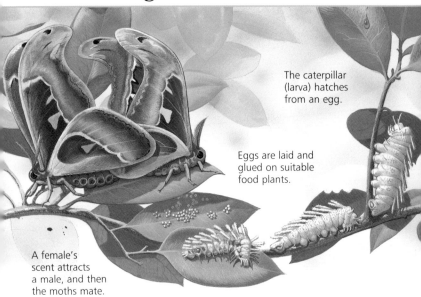

The caterpillar (larva) hatches from an egg.

Eggs are laid and glued on suitable food plants.

A female's scent attracts a male, and then the moths mate.

■ Eighty-five percent of all insect species alive today develop through a process of complete metamorphosis. The larvae look very different from the adult and they go through a single, dramatic transformation to adulthood.

EATING MACHINES

When the larvae hatch from eggs, they are soft-bodied, wingless, and often legless. The larvae of butterflies and moths are called caterpillars; those of beetles are called grubs; and the larvae of flies are called maggots. Larvae eat constantly. Their first meal is often their eggshell, which may contain chemicals to stimulate larval feeding. When fully grown (which may involve a series of molts), the larva stops eating in preparation for pupation. Many insects form pupal cases, and some build silk or earth cocoons for protection. During pupation,

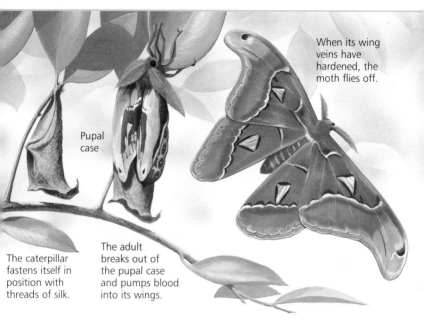

When its wing veins have hardened, the moth flies off.

Pupal case

The caterpillar fastens itself in position with threads of silk.

The adult breaks out of the pupal case and pumps blood into its wings.

LIFE CHANGES An atlas moth has four stages in its lifecycle—egg, larva, pupa and adult. Larvae put all effort into feeding, while adults mate and lay eggs.

the juvenile body starts to take on adult features. The fully mature adult emerges, complete with wings and reproductive organs. Adults look vastly different from their larval stages. They often eat different foods and live in completely different habitats.

LONG WAIT Jewel beetle larvae spend up to seven years burrowing through oak trees. They form a chamber in which to pupate and then emerge as adults.

Spider Young

■ Like insects, many spiders produce thousands of eggs, but very few survive through to adulthood. All spiders wrap their eggs in silk bundles called egg sacs or brood chambers. Many species can be identified by the color and design of their egg sac. The young break out of these sacs soon after they hatch, often clinging to each other or to their

SILK PURSE The black widow's eggs are wrapped in a silk case and attached to the web. She may lay up to 20 eggs.

mother's body. Young spiders, called spiderlings, are miniature versions of their parents. The majority molt for the first time safely inside the egg sac. Many leave the sac by using threads of silk as sails to launch themselves into the wind.

Maternal care Some spiders, scorpions, and some harvestmen and ticks guard their eggs and young from predators.

FIRST MEAL

Many female spiders die soon after they have laid their eggs. For some spiderlings, their mother's body is the first food they eat before they have to catch it for themselves. Their mother ensures them a safe meal, and an increased chance of survival at a vulnerable stage of life.

SECURE RIDE The egg sac of a female wolf spider is attached to her spinnerets. After hatching, the spiderlings climb up on their mother's abdomen and stay with her until their first molt.

CAMOUFLAGE

There are many examples of camouflage in all the major animal groups, but the insect and spider world provides some of the most spectacular. Camouflage is one of the simplest means of defense—but it can also be used as a tool in the deception and capture of prey.

DIFFERENT HUES

Simple camouflage relies on an animal's color (through a process of natural selection and evolution) blending in with the colors of its surroundings. Many bugs and spiders that live on flowers display colors that are a close match with their chosen vegetation. It can be difficult to spot them against a backdrop of similar color or texture.

Warning colors Insects not only use color to help conceal them, but many use vibrant hues to broadcast to a potential predator that they are dangerous to eat. Large numbers of beetles and butterflies sport bright warning colors to advertise that they are poisonous. Some non-poisonous species mimic these patterns and colors and, therefore, derive their mimic's defensive benefits.

SHAPES AND FORMS

An animal's shape or body form can betray it to a predator. Many insects and spiders have conquered this problem with specialized shapes, spines, and appendages that help them mimic dead leaves, thorns, seed pods, sticks, stones, and bird droppings.

HIDDEN AWAY The yucca moth's close association with the yucca plant is reflected in a body shape and color that help to conceal it from predators.

LEAFY DISGUISE The upper side of this butterfly's wings are colorful and brightly patterned. But when it comes to rest on a branch, it folds its wings to reveal the dull, brownish underside that looks not unlike a dead leaf.

NEW LEAF The long-legged leaf katydid's body shape and coloration help to camouflage it from predators. Stillness is an important component of the disguise.

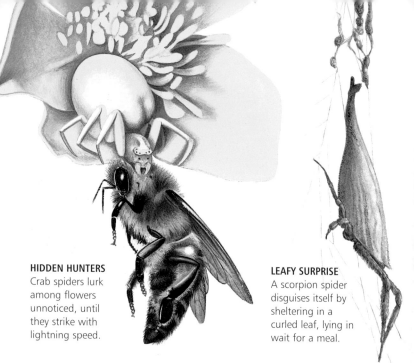

HIDDEN HUNTERS
Crab spiders lurk among flowers unnoticed, until they strike with lightning speed.

LEAFY SURPRISE
A scorpion spider disguises itself by sheltering in a curled leaf, lying in wait for a meal.

They carry this deception further by also copying the posture and other characteristics of the species or object they mimic. Many adult mantids resemble either green or dry leaves. When this is coupled with a to-and-fro movement similar to a leaf swaying in the wind, the mantid creates a formidable disguise. Insects may also mimic the body forms and postures of insects that are considered dangerous, particularly stinging insects, such as bees, ants, and wasps. Some beetle species hold their wings in a similar way to wasps, as well as walking in the same fashion. **Cover up** Many insects, especially young beetles and bugs, camouflage themselves by covering their bodies with sand, soil, or even their own excrement. Their body surface is often covered with hooks or bristles to help hold the materials in place.

Some species flatten themselves out against their background, using fringes of hairs to prevent them casting a shadow.

Group benefit Some butterfly, bee, wasp, and dragonfly species assemble in groups for resting. They cling to twigs or straws with their legs or mandibles, looking to a predator like a cluster of flowers on a plant.

SPIDER DISGUISE

Although most spiders can bite and inject venom, many employ camouflage to protect themselves from predators and to help them

STILL HIDING A significant part of this lichen spider's disguise is stillness. Many spiders also camouflage their egg sacs, with moss, leaves, and twigs.

catch prey. During the day, the female bird-dung spider looks, as its name suggests, like a bird's dropping. At night, it releases a chemical that mimics a female moth's scent, thus luring male moths and then eating them. Some Asian jumping spiders are nearly perfect mimics of a dangerous wasp species, complete with long spinnerets that look just like an wasp's antennae.

CAPTURING FOOD

Speed, good vision, strong jaws, stingers, and sometimes stealth and camouflage are the weapons used by predacious insects. Predators catch their prey by hunting actively, or by lying in wait until their victim comes within reach.

SPEED AND STEALTH

On the ground, active hunters include fast-moving beetles, as well as many ants and wasps. Tiger beetles have large, strong jaws, often armed with serrations to help them subdue prey. They are also among the fastest sprinters in the animal world.

GLOWING SUCCESS

The larvae of fungus gnats, a small fly found in caves in Australia and New Zealand, catch flying insects using light and sticky threads. Each luminescent larva produces a thread of sticky mucus that it suspends from the cave rock. This thread traps insects as they fly toward the glowing light. The larva then eats the insect and the trap.

Moving at more than 1½ feet (0.5 m) per second, they chase, grab, and crush ants in their jaws.

In the air, dragonflies swoop down and snatch up other flying insects with their long legs. Many other insects wait for prey to come to them, often by hiding in flowers or disguising themselves in foliage or leaf litter. Assassin bugs lurk among flowers, using their sharp proboscis to stab their victims and then suck out their body fluids.

Downhill run A few of these stationary hunters build special traps to catch their food. Antlion larvae dig steep-sided pits in loose soil and then wait for ants to tumble in.

Vision splendid Excellent eyesight is especially important for aerial predators, such as horseflies and dragonflies. The eyes of these groups are often larger and equipped with more acute vision than those of ground dwellers. This is probably the result of the fine adjustments that must be made when flying and hunting simultaneously.

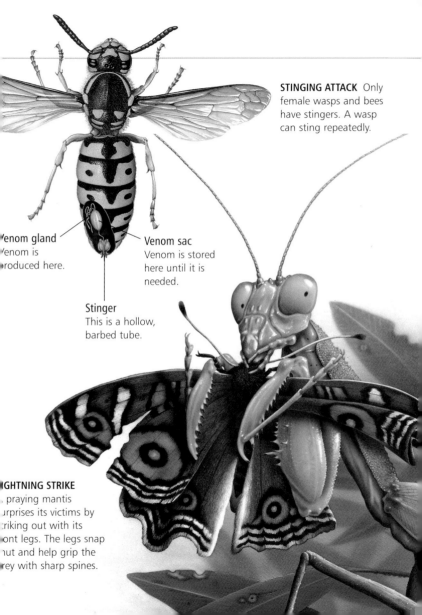

STINGING ATTACK Only female wasps and bees have stingers. A wasp can sting repeatedly.

Venom gland
Venom is produced here.

Venom sac
Venom is stored here until it is needed.

Stinger
This is a hollow, barbed tube.

LIGHTNING STRIKE
A praying mantis surprises its victims by striking out with its front legs. The legs snap shut and help grip the prey with sharp spines.

Weaving Webs

■ Spiders are the most versatile silk-makers in the world, and they are capable of making silk that has many uses. A spider's silk may be used to wrap prey and eggs, to line burrows, to make draglines for traveling, to produce sticky lines for prey capture, and to weave webs.

STRONG AS SILK

Spider silk is a liquid protein made in the silk glands. It is secreted from spigots on the spinnerets. The spider pulls out several strands at once and under tension the silk hardens. Spider silk is incredibly strong and elastic. Some giant orb-weaving spiders make webs strong enough to catch small birds.

Sticky traps Once a web is complete, spiders usually lie in wait, either on the web itself or close enough to touch it with their legs, and to sense vibrations.

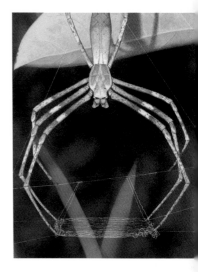

WEB DESIGN A net-throwing spider (above) holds its web with its legs, casting it over the prey. Spiders may wrap their prey to store it (opposite).

TAKING SHAPE Spiders' webs vary from extremely precise structures to untidy tangles. The shape of the web (right) can help to identify the owner.

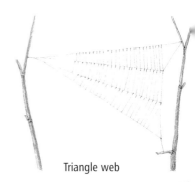

Triangle web

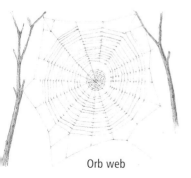

Orb web

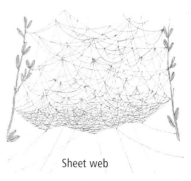

Sheet web

HUNTING FOR FOOD

Not all spiders catch their prey using webs. Many use traps of different kinds, while others actively seek their prey, pouncing on it when it comes into range.

STALKING SPIDERS

Spiders that search for food operate either by day or night. Because they are solitary hunters, most stake out their territory and defend the boundaries. Some wolf spiders chase off any intruder that tries to move in on their territory. Jumping spiders hunt mostly during the day. They are more free-roaming and leap after prey, trailing their silk drag lines behind them.

Ambushers Some spiders ambush their prey. Trapdoor spiders wait in their tunnels, just beneath a trapdoor made of silk, ready to pounce as soon as they detect vibrations in their trip wires. Others use camouflage to blend in with their surroundings, biding their time until an insect wanders into range. Some

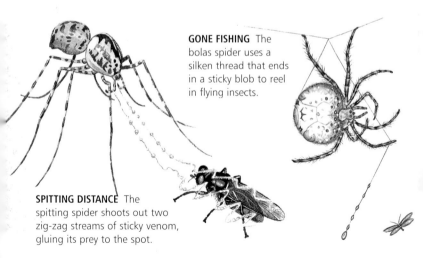

GONE FISHING The bolas spider uses a silken thread that ends in a sticky blob to reel in flying insects.

SPITTING DISTANCE The spitting spider shoots out two zig-zag streams of sticky venom, gluing its prey to the spot.

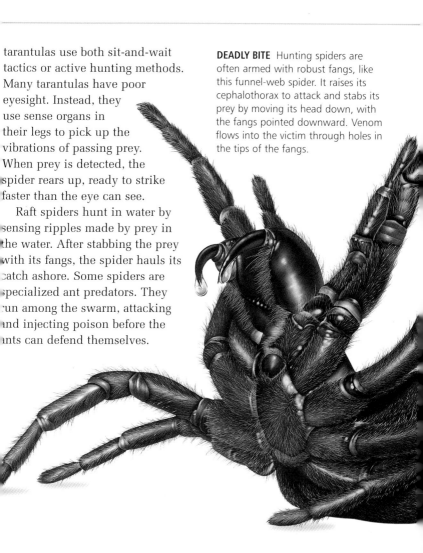

tarantulas use both sit-and-wait tactics or active hunting methods. Many tarantulas have poor eyesight. Instead, they use sense organs in their legs to pick up the vibrations of passing prey. When prey is detected, the spider rears up, ready to strike faster than the eye can see.

Raft spiders hunt in water by sensing ripples made by prey in the water. After stabbing the prey with its fangs, the spider hauls its catch ashore. Some spiders are specialized ant predators. They run among the swarm, attacking and injecting poison before the ants can defend themselves.

DEADLY BITE Hunting spiders are often armed with robust fangs, like this funnel-web spider. It raises its cephalothorax to attack and stabs its prey by moving its head down, with the fangs pointed downward. Venom flows into the victim through holes in the tips of the fangs.

EAT OR BE EATEN

Insects are under constant threat of being preyed upon by birds, lizards, spiders, and other insects. Many defend themselves by retreating from danger or by staying still and well hidden. They hide in soil or rotting wood, or make themselves look like the objects around them. Some harmless insects imitate those that are unpalatable or mimic those with dangerous stings.

LINES OF DEFENSE
If all other defenses fail, some insects stand their ground and attack. Some have armored bodies, sharp jaws, or toxic chemicals to deter a predator just long enough to make an escape.

Bush crickets exude droplets of foul-smelling liquid from their thorax to repel attackers. The bombardier beetle blasts hot, caustic substances at predators from a chamber in its abdomen. The bloody-nosed beetle breaks thin membranes in its mouth and forces out a droplet of its own blood. The blood of this beetle contains chemicals that make its attacker very ill.

Copycats Monarch butterflies are poisonous and their bright orange colors advertise this well. The harmless viceroy butterfly mimics the monarch's colors and patterns, hoodwinking predators into believing it to be toxic also.

Startling flash Some bugs and katydids startle intruders by flashing normally concealed eyespots or brilliant colors, giving them a chance to make a getaway.

EYES AND SPOTS Many moths sport large eyespots on their wings (left). These may startle a predator by making the moth appear to have a large, threatening face. Ladybugs (right) warn enemies of their bitter taste with bright colors and spots.

ON GUARD The puss moth caterpillar raises its head and flicks two rear whips from side to side when it is disturbed. As a last resort, it sprays formic acid.

Five-spotted ladybug

Ten-spotted ladybug

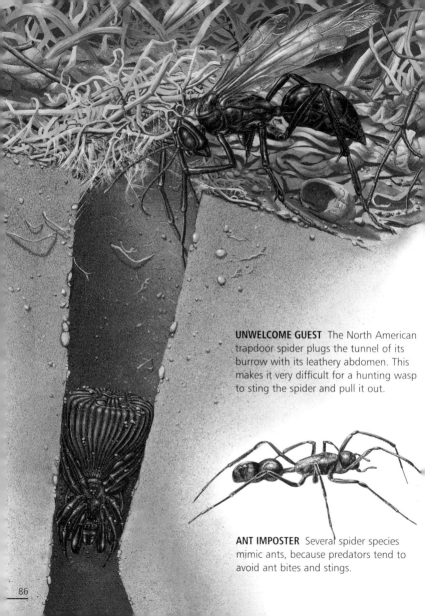

UNWELCOME GUEST The North American trapdoor spider plugs the tunnel of its burrow with its leathery abdomen. This makes it very difficult for a hunting wasp to sting the spider and pull it out.

ANT IMPOSTER Several spider species mimic ants, because predators tend to avoid ant bites and stings.

SPIDER DEFENSE

Spiders are vulnerable to attack from many different animals, mostly birds, lizards, toads, and small mammals. They may also be attacked by parasitic insects, such as the ichneumon wasp, and from members of their own species.

Out of sight Many spiders have developed strategies to avoid being eaten. Some conceal themselves by lurking in burrows or burying themselves in sand. A few will suddenly drop out of their web, dangling from a safety line. Others escape notice by camouflaging themselves or by mimicking a more dangerous animal.

Spiny-backed spiders have unusually hard and spiky abdomens. This is thought to be a defense against predation by birds. Some spiders display their toxicity by having bright red markings to warn off potential predators. Large South American tarantulas are known to flick microscopic barbed hairs, which irritate the skin of their attackers.

LOOSE LEGS In response to danger, some spiders shed a leg to confuse a predator, and then make their escape.

FOOD AND FEEDING

As a group, insects devour a vast range of different foods. Individual species may have highly specialized requirements, and specially adapted mouthparts for procuring and eating food. Often larval stages have very different food requirements and feeding habits to the adults. In some species, adults may not feed at all, depending on the reserves stored in the larval stage.

DIFFERENT FOOD

Many insects are predators, killing and eating other animals to survive. Predators do not require as much food as plant-eaters because their meals provide significantly more protein and nutrition. The mouthparts of these insects are often equipped with strong, sharp mandibles.

Vegetarians and bloodsuckers

Plant-eating insects have mouthparts ideal for cutting, tearing, shredding, or drilling into their food. Many species feed exclusively on sap, nectar, or other plant liquids. These insects have mouthparts that can suck or sponge up liquid. Parasites, such as fleas and some flies, have specialized mouthparts for drinking blood from their hosts.

GNAWING HUNGER An acorn weevil has the perfect proboscis for boring through tough nuts. Jaws on the tip of the snout can gnaw on the seed inside the acorn.

NECTAR SIPPER
The hairy bee fly has long, needlelike mouthparts, which it uses to drink nectar from flowers.

MOUTHPARTS
A grasshopper's strong jaws have sharp edges for cutting tough grasses. Carnivorous tiger beetles have toothed jaws to catch, subdue, and cut up prey.

Grasshopper
Herbivore

Tiger beetle
Carnivore

DANGEROUS MEAL

The larvae and adults of monarch butterflies are poisonous to eat and are avoided by most predators. The larvae feed on a highly toxic plant called milkweed, with no ill-effects. In fact, the larvae incorporate the milkweed's poisons into their own body tissues, which also makes their flesh poisonous. During metamorphosis, this chemical defense is passed on to the adult. Most insects that store plant poisons have bright colors and patterns to warn predators of this peril.

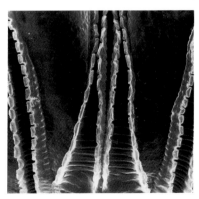

LIQUID LUNCH This close-up of a housefly's tongue shows the structures that help them mop up their liquid food.

ARACHNID FOOD

Arachnids cannot ingest solid food. To be able to eat their prey, they begin to break it down before it reaches their digestive system.

Deadly bite Most hunting spiders bite and inject poison and digestive juices into their prey simultaneously. Web-making spiders usually wrap their prey first, to help immobilize it before they deliver the deadly bite. Spider families with stabbing fangs (mygalomorphs) inject digestive juice into their prey by piercing through the skin of their prey, and suck the body fluids out through the same holes. As a consequence, their prey looks outwardly undamaged. Spider families with laterally moveable fangs (araneomorphs) tear their food while they pour in digestive juice. The remains of their prey are totally unrecognizable.

SLOW EATERS After this *Dysdera* spider has immobilized its prey with venom, it may take twelve hours to digest it. It may store its catch until it is ready to feed.

Scorpions Scorpions use their modified pedipalps to catch prey, and then subdue it by injecting poison from their tail stinger. Some have powerful venom that can cause respiratory and muscle paralysis. Once the prey is dead, they digest it in a similar way to spiders, breaking it down before it enters the digestive system.

Ticks and mites Ticks and mites use their specialized chelicerae to feed on skin, blood, and body tissues. Some ticks feed on a host for as little as an hour; others may

SUCKING UP Scorpions digest their prey by reducing the victim's tissues to a soupy consistency. They then suck up the liquid into their mouth.

feed for up to six months. They inject an anti-coagulant to help the blood flow freely. When fully engorged, they simply drop off the host. In most cases, the initial bite and penetration of the tick is not felt by the victim. Some mites have chelicerae that are adapted for cutting through skin or for eating body tissue or lymph.

LIVING TOGETHER

The majority of insects and spiders live solitary lives, only coming together to mate, or to feed at a common food source. Truly "social" species—termites, ants, and some wasps and bees—cooperate to find food, build the nest, take care of young, and defend the colony from attack. Many generations may exist in the same nest at the same time.

LABOR DIVIDED

Members of colonies are divided into strictly defined "castes"—usually a queen, drones, workers, and soldiers—each with a specific role. Male drones mate with the queen, who produces all the eggs. The workers collect food and care for the eggs and young. Ant and termite colonies have soldiers to protect them from intruders. All this behavior is instinctively led—no one individual directs the others. Together, their efforts add up to a better chance of survival for the colony as a whole.

Building together Most social insects construct special nests to protect their young. In social bees

PAPER HOME Social insects cooperate to build shelters for their developing young, and for the rest of the colony. Social wasps construct layered, paper nests.

and wasps, nests consist of many hexagonal cells. The ingenious hexagonal shape allows for the maximum number of cells to be packed into the smallest area. Ants and termites construct a nest above or under the ground, often made up of a maze of tunnels and chambers. Here, the eggs are laid, the young are fed and protected, and in some cases, food is cultivated for the colony.

TOTAL CONTROL

Within the nest, the queen controls the reproductive status of her workers by exuding pheromones to prevent them from breeding. Queen ants, wasps, and bees can also determine the sex of their offspring. They withhold sperm stored in their body if male offspring are preferred, because males are produced from unfertilized eggs. Fertilized eggs become females.

Bees and Wasps

■ Some of the best-known wasps and bees, such as hornets, bumblebees, and honeybees, are social insects. They are vital to most ecosystems as pollinators, parasites, and predators. These social species collaborate to build sometimes elaborate nests in which to raise their young.

HIGH SOCIETY

Social bees live in colonies consisting of a queen, female workers, and male drones. They nest in hollow trees or human-made hives, constructing a water-resistant, waxen comb made up of a matrix of hexagonal cells. The cells provide a chamber for the developing larvae, as well as storage bins for honey that can feed the colony when nectar and flowers are scarce.

The reproductive female, or queen, is the head of the colony, and she produces all the larvae—sometimes more than 50,000 in her 5 years of life. The purpose of the short-lived drones, which develop from unfertilized eggs, is to mate with the queen. Worker bees build the nest, attend to the young, and gather food for the whole hive.

Wasps Most social wasps have similar social structures to bees. Many build nests using layers of chewed wood "paper." Hornets make their nests in hollow trees. Their colonies consist of only a few hundred workers.

NEW DIRECTION Honeybees communicate information to nestmates using a special dance. A fast abdomen waggle means plenty of nectar, and the direction of the dance tells nestmates where to locate it.

BEE YOUNG Worker bees bring food to the larvae as they mature inside their wax cells. These larvae are transforming into pupae, and will then emerge as adults.

COMMUNITY WORK Social bee larvae are fed bee bread—a mixture of honey and pollen—by the workers. Royal jelly is reserved for the queen's daughter.

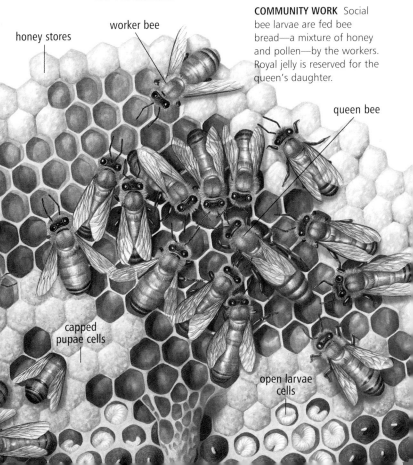

honey stores

worker bee

queen bee

capped pupae cells

open larvae cells

Termites

■ Termites live in permanent social colonies and have distinct castes: the queen, the king, soldiers, and workers. Workers build the nest, forage for food, and tend the young. Soldiers have larger heads than the workers, and they produce repellent secretions to ward off attackers.

ROYAL SWARM

Winged reproductive termites spend their life in the cool of the nest, eating the food collected by the workers. Thousands leave their nests on warm evenings, swarming in the air in search of a partner. After landing, a king and queen break off their wings and mate. Depending on the species, they excavate a cell below the soil's surface in which the first worker nymphs are hatched. These workers undergo an incomplete metamorphosis, and then begin extending the nest by constructing a network of tunnels and chambers. Unlike the workers of social bees and ants, which are all female, worker termites can be sterile males and females.

WOOD DIGESTION Termites and their young eat wood fibers. Their digestive tracts contain bacteria that secrete enzymes capable of digesting cellulose.

Good foundations The royal cell is the foundation of a termite nest. The only fertile male in the colony, the king lives beside the queen, who can lay an egg every few seconds. The king and queen may live for more than ten years and produce millions of eggs. Radiating out from the royal cell are the larval chambers, where the eggs and nymphs are cared for by the workers.

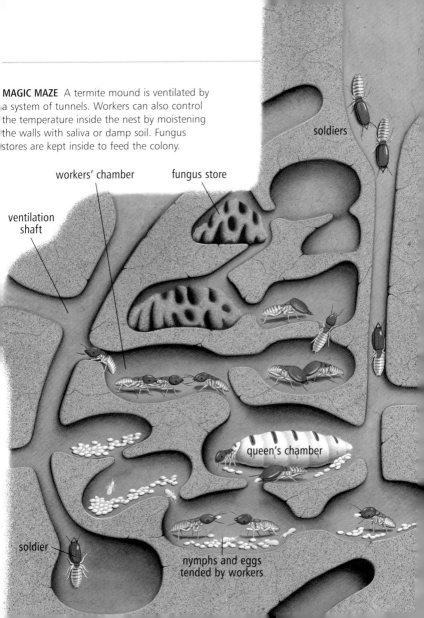

MAGIC MAZE A termite mound is ventilated by a system of tunnels. Workers can also control the temperature inside the nest by moistening the walls with saliva or damp soil. Fungus stores are kept inside to feed the colony.

soldiers

workers' chamber

fungus store

ventilation shaft

queen's chamber

soldier

nymphs and eggs tended by workers

Ants

■ All 9,000 species of ant are social insects. They live in colonies divided into castes and are controlled by a queen. Most ants build their nests in wood or plants, or out of soil.

CASTE OUT

There are two castes of ants within most colonies—the queen and the workers, who are all female. The few males in the colony exist only to mate with a new queen in order to start a new nest. The young winged queen flies from her old nest and mates once with a winged male. After biting off her wings, she starts a nest that is then extended by her female offspring.

Scent trails Like social bees, ants use pheromones to identify themselves, and to communicate with each other. Pheromones are used by the queen to sterilize the workers, and workers leave pheromone trails to guide other ants to food or to the nest.

On guard When a nest is attacked, workers rush to defend it. They attack in great numbers, biting the enemy with their powerful jaws.

COMPOST FACTORY Leaf-cutter ants snip fragments from leaves and carry them back to their nest. There, the fragments are chewed and inserted into mounds of fungus. The fungus breaks down the leaf fibers into food for the ants.

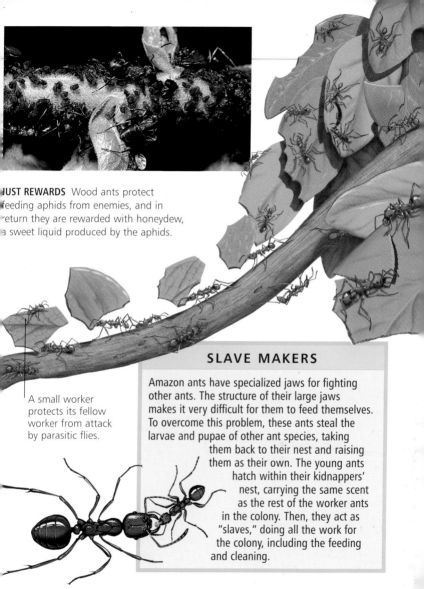

JUST REWARDS Wood ants protect feeding aphids from enemies, and in return they are rewarded with honeydew, a sweet liquid produced by the aphids.

A small worker protects its fellow worker from attack by parasitic flies.

SLAVE MAKERS

Amazon ants have specialized jaws for fighting other ants. The structure of their large jaws makes it very difficult for them to feed themselves. To overcome this problem, these ants steal the larvae and pupae of other ant species, taking them back to their nest and raising them as their own. The young ants hatch within their kidnappers' nest, carrying the same scent as the rest of the worker ants in the colony. Then, they act as "slaves," doing all the work for the colony, including the feeding and cleaning.

Fantastic Journeys

■ At certain times of the year, the air may be teeming with insects on the move. Some are escaping adverse seasonal conditions; others are on their way to colonize new habitats.

AERIAL EPICS

Many butterflies and moths undertake long journeys to escape the cold weather in winter and to find favorable feeding places in warmer climes. The painted lady butterfly occurs in temperate and tropical regions. Some specimens have been seen over the Atlantic and Indian oceans, more than 500 miles (800 km) from land. During warmer years, they may even cross the Arctic Circle.

Compass bearings Most butterflies are believed to navigate using the Sun. They stay at a constant angle to the Sun, following a curved arc as it moves across the sky.

The major compass cue for migrating moths is the moon. On nights when the moon is not

DRIVER'S SEAT A colony of hundreds of thousands of driver ants moves across the forest floor in search of a more favorable nest site. The eggs, larvae, and queen are carried and fed as they go.

LEAVING HOME When a beehive reaches a certain size, it must divide in order to survive. A new queen emerges from a queen cell within the hive; the old queen leaves, surrounded by a swarm of workers and some drones.

visible, moths may orient themselves by the stars, and by Earth's magnetic field.

Vast numbers Locusts are usually solitary insects. But if food becomes scarce, they may band together in huge swarms, some containing several billion insects, and then take to the air in search of food. Some desert locusts embark on sea crossings, and have been found on ships far from land. Others undertake journeys of 3,000 miles (5,000 km) in five days or less.

LONG HAUL Millions of monarch butterflies travel thousands of miles from North America to Mexico to avoid the freezing winter conditions.

Spiders on the Move

■ Unlike most insects that rely on their wings to carry them to new habitats, spiders and other arachnids use different techniques to help them leave the nest and colonize new lands.

HITCHHIKERS

The spiderlings of many species use threads as sails to launch themselves into the wind from the tops of plants. Others use a technique called ballooning to hitch a ride on the wind. The spiderling stands on tiptoe in an exposed position, such as the end of a branch. It faces the wind and squeezes out a droplet of silk. Pulled by the wind, the droplet expands into threads, and the spiderling floats away. Some spiders travel hundreds of miles in this way, carried by wind currents. Some have been found during aerial surveys at altitudes of up to 3 miles (5 km).

Lucky landings Because of their small size and relative lightness, most spiders are afforded a safe landing after their aerial journey. However, many perish when the breeze drops them in adverse environments, such as the ocean, where they either drown, or become food for fishes.

Easy riders Other arachnids employ different methods to move them from place to place. Pseudoscorpions and mites attach themselves to flying insects or birds, or to the fur of a passing mammal. Wherever the host goes, its cargo travels also.

ON A THREAD The unique "ballooning" technique used by some spiderlings allows them to be carried away on silken threads.

DRAGLINE DROP Some spiderlings leave their nest by climbing to a high perch and dropping a dragline. When the dragline breaks, the spider drifts gently to the ground.

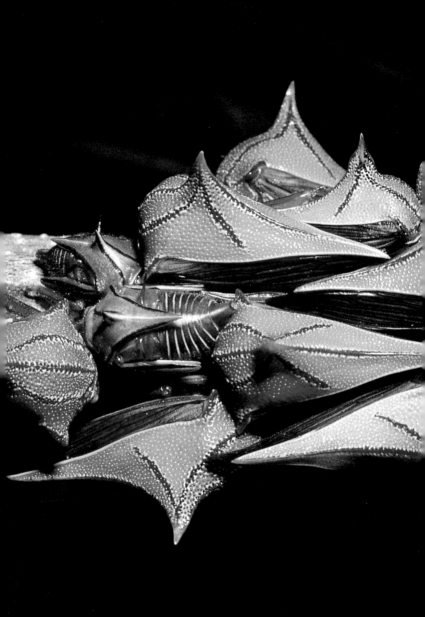

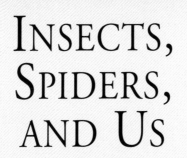

INSECTS,
SPIDERS,
AND US

*An investigation of the
relationship between people and
insects and spiders*

Friend or Foe?

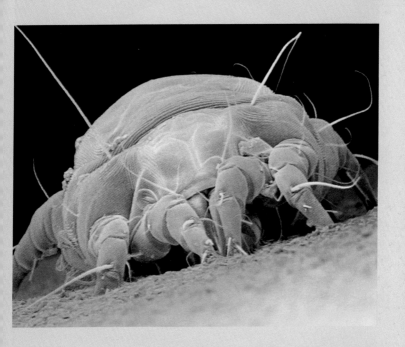

MANY HUMANS FEAR AND LOATHE insects and spiders. Some carry diseases and destroy important food crops. A few can even deliver a fatal sting or bite. Flea-borne bubonic plague decimated Europe's population during the 1300s, and malaria, carried by mosquitoes, is still reponsible for thousands of deaths every year. Humans, in turn, have had a huge impact on insect and spider populations. Habitat destruction, in particular, has seen the numbers of some species dwindle to dangerously low levels.

CROP DESTRUCTION

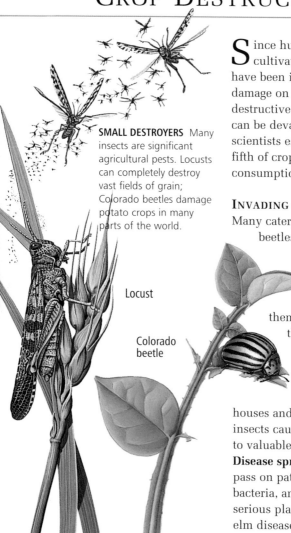

SMALL DESTROYERS Many insects are significant agricultural pests. Locusts can completely destroy vast fields of grain; Colorado beetles damage potato crops in many parts of the world.

Locust

Colorado beetle

S ince humans began to cultivate plants, there have been insects inflicting damage on their crops. The destructive power of insects can be devastating for farmers: scientists estimate that about one-fifth of crops grown for human consumption are eaten by insects.

INVADING HORDES

Many caterpillars, bugs, and beetles attack valuable food crops. Swarms of locusts can descend on fields, stripping them bare of grain in less than an hour. Weevils and meal moths bore through stored grain; beetles and termites bore through wood in houses and furniture; and some insects cause illness and irritation to valuable livestock.

Disease spreaders Insects may pass on pathogens, such as fungi, bacteria, and viruses, that cause serious plant diseases. Dutch elm disease, which affects the

American elm tree, is transmitted by the elm bark beetle. This beetle carries on its body the spores of the fungi that cause the disease.

Skin deep The kind of damage inflicted on a plant depends largely on the mouthparts the invading insect possesses. Chewing is the most visible form of destruction, but piercing and sucking of plant fluids probably inflicts the most devastation.

DESERT STORM A swarm of desert locusts may contain more than 40 billion individuals. Usually solitary insects, locusts gather in huge swarms when food is scarce, eating tons of green plant matter.

Many insects damage plants and fruits through egg-laying scars and nest building. Discoloration caused by scale insects can also reduce the commercial value of many fruit and vegetable crops.

DISEASE CARRIERS

Insects carry many diseases that are harmful to humans and animals. As a result, disease-carrying insects have played an integral role in shaping human history. Until the widespread use of insecticides, and the development of antibiotics and inoculations, twice as many soldiers were struck down by insect-transmitted diseases than were killed during armed conflict.

WORLD SHAPERS

The most serious disease spread by insects is malaria. Female mosquitoes feed on animal blood, and also carry the malaria parasite, called *Plasmodium*, in their salivary glands. Throughout history, malaria has had a major impact on human health. Today, it remains the number one killer of humans throughout the world, and is still responsible for killing between two to four million people every year. Scientists estimate that about half the world's population, mostly in the tropics, either have malaria or are in danger of contracting it. Other

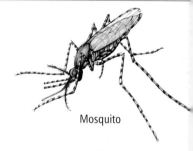

Mosquito

mosquito-borne diseases include yellow fever, dengue fever, and encephalitis. An outbreak of yellow fever in the late 1800s delayed the building of the Panama Canal and killed approximately 18,000 workers.

Lice, mites, and ticks Lice are ectoparasites and most cause irritation and blood loss to their chosen host. Human body lice can also transmit epidemic typhus, especially in times of population stress, and during war and famine.

Dust mites feed on the dead skin and hair cells humans shed

PROBLEM FEEDERS Dust mites (top right) cause allergic reactions, including asthma Deer ticks (bottom right) carry the bacteria that cause Lyme disease. Symptoms include rashes and fever.

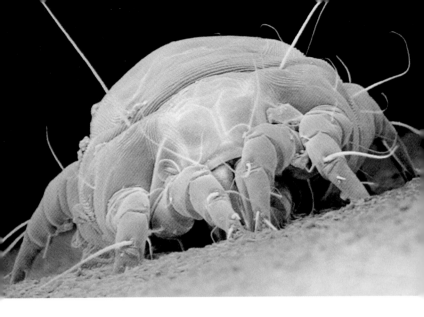

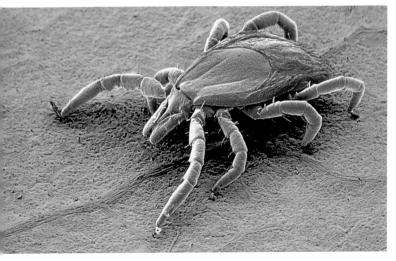

in their thousands every day. Some people are allergic to dust mite droppings, and may suffer from asthma if they inhale them. Some mite species cause severe cases of dermatitis and other allergic reactions.

Many ticks transmit serious diseases to poultry, cattle, sheep, and horses, as well as to domestic pets, such as dogs. They may also carry viruses that cause encephalitis, tick typhus, and Lyme disease in humans.

Black death World epidemics of bubonic plague killed millions of people and, as a consequence, changed the structure of society. The plague, or black death, swept through Europe in the Middle Ages. Between 1346 and 1350, one-third of the population died from this disease, which was spread by fleas living on the black rats of Asia.

Flies on us At present, flies are by far the greatest disease-transmitters of all. House flies passively spread many illnesses, including typhoid, cholera, and gastroenteritis. They walk over feces, rubbish, and other waste products, spreading germs as they go.

The tsetse fly of Africa spreads the trypanosome parasite that causes the debilitating disease known as sleeping sickness. The flies bite infected animals and then pass it on to humans.

FATAL FLEAS Outbreaks of bubonic plague devastated the population of Europe in the 1300s. This 15th century painting from the Toggenberg bible depicts patients suffering from the disease. Fleas were the major vector, feeding on infected rats, and then biting humans.

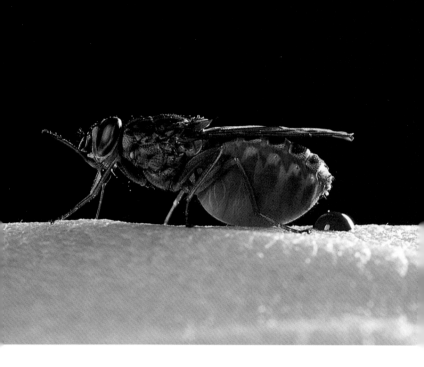

FIRST BLOOD The tsetse fly (above), which feeds on the blood of cattle and humans, can gorge itself until it is hugely swollen. It spreads sleeping sickness disease that affects the nervous system of animals and humans. Ticks (right) often feed in clusters on host animals. They transmit many diseases, including encephalitis and Lyme disease.

ENDANGERED SPECIES

Insects and spiders are vital components of our global ecosystems. In fact, most ecosystems would cease to function without insect and spider species. Earth's biodiversity will be changed forever if humans continue to change and destroy their habitat.

WAR OF THE WORLDS

Chemical insecticides, herbicides, and fertilizers indirectly threaten biodiversity by contaminating air and groundwater. Insecticides kill

COLLECTING JEWELS Many birdwing butterflies are highly prized by collectors. This, coupled with shrinking habitat, has seen the disappearance of many species.

not only the targeted species, but many harmless species as well. Eventually, plants and animals that rely on these insects for pollination, and as a food source, are also adversely affected.

Urban crawl The pressures of rural and urban development have taken their toll. For example, the Texan tooth cave spider is under threat because many of the caves it inhabited have been filled in.

Worth saving Insect and spiders are worth preserving. The best way to protect insect and spider diversity is to preserve habitat. Some countries have also introduced legislation to protect international trade in vulnerable species.

CREEPING THREAT The collection of spiders for pets has endangered some species. The Mexican red-kneed tarantula (left) is now protected by law.

Good Friends

MANY HUMANS IGNORE THE ENORMOUS benefits that insects
and spiders bring to our lives. Without bees, beetles, and
other vital pollinators, many food crops would be unable to
produce their fruits or seeds. Useful products, such as honey,
silk, dyes, and medicines are all derived from insects. Many
species help to maintain the health of our ecosystems. This
chapter includes information on how to observe and study
insects and spiders safely, helping to increase our
knowledge and enjoyment of these fascinating creatures.

VENOMS AND MEDICINES

Venoms are complex combinations of chemicals that, drop for drop, are among the most toxic substances known. Some insects and many arachnids produce these compounds inside modified salivary glands or vestigial reproductive organs. To help them subdue their prey, and to protect themselves from enemies, they inject their poison using their fangs, stingers, or piercing mouthparts.

DANGEROUS COCKTAIL

Venoms have many effects on the body systems of animals. Some of the most common symptoms are pain, paralysis, interference with blood clotting, and the breakdown of heart and lung tissue.

Male Sydney funnel-web spiders are the only male spiders with venomous bites that are dangerous to humans. Dogs, cats, and other mammals appear to be relatively resistant to their poison. A funnel-web's bite can cause extreme illness, or even death, in a relatively short time. Before an antivenin was developed, many children died from this spider's bite.

The saliva of the Australian paralysis tick contains a toxin that causes progressive paralysis in some humans and a severe allergic reaction in others.

ANT POWER

venom duct

stinger

Australia's bulldog ants are the largest, and among the most dangerous ants, in the world. As few as 30 stings from these aggressive ants can kill a human. Those allergic to the venom may suffer life-threatening reactions also. They inject their poison using a stinger on their abdomen.

The North African scorpion is the most deadly of all scorpions. Its venom attacks the nervous system and may cause death within minutes of a sting.

Antidote solution Venom is collected from spiders, ticks and other poisonous creatures to help develop medicines, or antivenins, to counteract the effects of toxic bites. Antivenins are available for some scorpion, ant, spider, and bee venoms.

GOOD BITE To produce an antivenin, funnel-web spiders are first milked for their venom. The venom is injected into a bite-resistant mammal and the antibodies it produces are purified for use.

Good use Venom research is helping in the development of medicines for illnesses, such as cancer and multiple sclerosis. Honeybee venom may be used to alleviate the symptoms of arthritis and other inflammatory diseases.

USEFUL PRODUCERS

Humans rely on insects to provide them with a wide range of useful products. Insects make honey and wax, oils and silks, natural medicines and dyes. In some countries, insects provide a valuable protein food source for humans. Insects are important in crop production as plant-pollinators. Insects are also useful subjects in scientific research.

SOFT TOUCH Silkworm caterpillars are fed a diet of fresh mulberry leaves. When they pupate, their cocoons are carefully tended by silk farm workers.

SWEET AS HONEY

As well as being Earth's major pollinators, honeybees produce valuable honey and beeswax. In order to produce 1 pound (500 g) of honey, bees may fly more than 5,600 miles (9,000 km). A single hive can produce 110 pounds (50 kg) of honey per year, which means they have traveled more than 615,000 miles (1 million km) in total.

Weaving threads Silk is made from the material that silkworm caterpillars use to spin their cocoon. Although commercial silk is produced by a number of species, most comes from the cocoons of the domesticated commercial silkworm moth from Asia. This moth is now used in silk farms all over the world.

When the caterpillars are ready to pupate, they produce saliva that solidifies into thread when it comes into contact with the air. Silkworm caterpillars take approximately three days to spin their cocoons. Once finished, the the cocoons are baked in an oven to kill the insects inside. They are

IN THE BOX Beekeepers place the queen honeybee inside the hive. Honeybee workers seek the queen out, relocating to the same hive to attend to her needs.

SILKEN THREADS Each silk moth cocoon (left) is made from a single silk thread more than 1/2 mile (1 km) long. Silk thread is the strongest natural fiber.

then dropped in boiling water, causing them to unravel into single strands. The single strands are twisted together to make silk thread, and this is then woven into cloth.

Useful variety Several other insects make products that are important to humans. Certain dyes are produced by scale insects—the Asian lac insect, for example, produces substances used in the manufacture of varnishes, such as shellac.

Control agents Predacious insects are now widely used as biological control agents, particularly for insecticide-free crop protection and pest control in domestic gardens. Ladybugs may control aphids that are harmful to many garden plants and vegetable crops. Dung beetles help to decompose the droppings of domestic stock.

Pollination Partnership

■ Insects and flowering plants evolved side by side over millions of years. During this time, some insects became plant-eaters or sap-suckers; others struck valuable partnerships with plants to become their primary pollinators. Many plants are unable to reproduce without the services of their insect partners.

FREQUENT FLIERS

Most flowering plants rely on insects to carry their pollen from one flower to another. Insects, such as honeybees, visit flowers

FLOWER FEAST Beetles carry pollen on their bodies as they move from flower to flower in order to feed. They are attracted to flowers by color and scent.

in search of sugary sweet nectar and pollen. A dusting of pollen grains gets caught on the bee's body as it brushes against the flower's stamens. Some of this pollen rubs off on the stigma of the next flower the bee visits, fertilizing the plant in a process called cross-pollination. Bees rely on the plant's bounty as a food source for the colony; in turn, the plant relies on cross-pollination to bear viable fruit and seeds.

Some plants have evolved flowers that mimic the shape and coloration of a female wasp. When the male attempts to mate with the flower, it receives a dusting of pollen instead.

Bearing fruit One in every three bites we eat is produced thanks to the services of an insect or some other pollinator. Some of the valuable crops that require insect pollination include apples, pears, onions, and potatoes.

SPECIAL DELIVERY
Honeybees deliver pollen to flowers as they collect food for their hive.

INSECT AND SPIDER STUDIES

The best way to understand insects and spiders is to observe them firsthand. Taking the time to study their everyday lives can be a rewarding experience. The most important tools of observation are your eyes and ears. Learn to look and listen closely—the smallest details are often the most fascinating.

UP CLOSE A plastic or glass jar with holes punched in the lid makes a good observation chamber. Provide some moisture using a damp tissue in a dish, and add leaves or twigs. When you have finished, release the insect where you originally found it.

INSECT COLLECTING

Insects and spiders can be observed in their natural habitat, or they can be collected for closer inspection before being returned to their environment. Take a few minutes to listen and look carefully: detecting the presence of cleverly camouflaged animals, such as katydids, may depend almost entirely on aural signs.

Closer look To extend your vision, a hand lens and magnifying glass are valuable pieces of field equipment. A 35 mm single lens reflex camera (SLR) may assist you in recording your observations. A macro lens (50–100 mm) will help ensure well-focussed results.

Identifying insects Once you have collected interesting specimens, identifying them, especially to order level, can be relatively easy with some practice and an appropriate field guide.

Welcome visitors One of the best ways to observe insects and spiders is to attract them to the garden. A diverse range of habitats and vegetation will attract a diverse range of insects.

LOOK AND NOTE A magnifying glass can help to zero in on intricate details. Sketching is a satisfying way to record your observations.

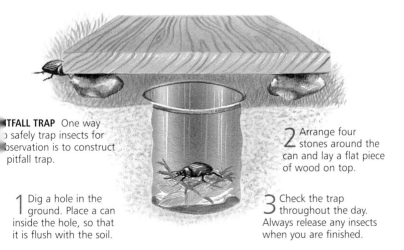

PITFALL TRAP One way to safely trap insects for observation is to construct a pitfall trap.

1 Dig a hole in the ground. Place a can inside the hole, so that it is flush with the soil.

2 Arrange four stones around the can and lay a flat piece of wood on top.

3 Check the trap throughout the day. Always release any insects when you are finished.

KINDS OF INSECTS

*An informative, illustrated guide
to the major orders of insects,
and their relatives*

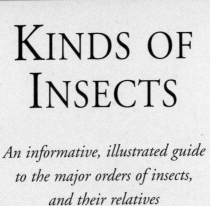

USING THE GUIDE

This guide gives informative and detailed descriptions of the world's major insect and arachnid groups. It is divided into two parts and five main chapters. Each chapter covers an important group of orders, each of which have key characteristics in common. Most entries are arranged by order, although suborders are included, when required, to increase clarity.

The characteristics, life cycle, diet, and habitat for an order or suborder are outlined in each entry. With more than 1,000 families worldwide, each entry includes descriptions of representative or well-known families only.

Illustrations and photographs show the form, coloration, and sometimes behavioral aspects of selected species.

Within the chapters, orders are listed in taxonomic sequence.

The sample page opposite shows the typical layout of an order entry, and is annotated to show the main features.

The order to which the families belong.

The number of families in the order. When a suborder further defines an order, it is listed here.

The common name of each order or suborder.

HYMENOPTERA
91 families

Bees, Wasps, Ants, and Sawflies

Number of species: 198,000

Length: $^1/_{128}$–$2^3/_4$ in (0.25–70 mm)

■ CHARACTERISTICS
Hymenopterans are vital plant pollinators, predators, and parasites in the world's ecosystems. Many species in this large order are also social insects. All adults have chewing mouthparts, which for some species act as tools for digging building nests, and slicing u

SNAPSHOT

ORDER FEATURES Usually constricted "waist" between thorax and abdomen, fore and hindwings joined by chewing mouthparts; mat groups are social
DIET Insect and plant ma
LIFE CYCLE Metamorpho complete; eggs laid in n
HABITAT All terrestrial h
DISTRIBUTION Worldwid

248 KINDS OF INSECTS

The approximate number of known species worldwide within the order.

The range of body lengths or wingspans for each order.

Snapshot panels give vital at-a-glance information about each order, including diagnostic features, diet, life cycle, habitat, and distribution.

Photographs and illustrations of representative families within the order are a visual aid to the text descriptions.

...g bee is a vital
...ng flowers. Pollen
...hairs as it feeds.

...wo pairs of
...gs that join
...all hooks during
...compound eyes.
...on of sawflies,
...abdomen are
...nstricted "waist,"
...l. The ovipositor
... ants, and social
...lved into a stinger
...d poison glands.
...ns range in size
...fly wasp, so small
...rough the eye of a
...e spider-eating wasp,
...³/₄ inches (70 mm).

...CLE AND DIET
...opterans undergo
...metamorphosis.
...eggs produce females

NO SWEAT
Also called sweat bees,
members of the family
Halictidae brood their eggs
underground, within cells
that are waterproofed with
a special bee secretion.

LEAF-CUTTERS
Female leaf-cutter bees clip
out circular pieces of leaf
with their jaws. These are
taken back to their nests
where they are fashioned
into tube-shaped cells for
the eggs and larvae.

WINGED INSECTS 249

Captions provide
extra information on
a representative species
within an order.

Main text describes the principal
characteristics of the order or
suborder. Subsequent sub-
headings and text describe the
characteristics of well-known
or representative families.

Primitive Wingless Insects

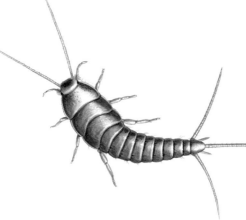

OFTEN MINUTE IN SIZE AND SECRETIVE IN HABITS, these insects may go unnoticed, and are sadly understudied. They do not undergo an obvious metamorphosis, but instead molt to increase their size at certain periods throughout their lives. These insects play an essential role in Earth's ecosystems and are important links in food chains. They are prey items for many larger invertebrates, including other insects, and spiders and their relatives.

PROTURA

4 families

Proturans

Number of species: 400

Length: 1/64–1/16 in (0.5–2 mm)

COLLEMBOLA

18 families

Springtails

Number of species: 6,500

Length: 1/32–5/16 in (1–8 mm)

DIPLURA

9 families

Diplurans

Number of species: 800

Length: 1/4–1 1/4 in (6–30 mm)

■ PROTURANS
Characteristics Proturans are primitive, pale, wingless, and blind. They do not possess antennae. The front pair of legs have a sensory function. The piercing and sucking mouthparts are concealed inside a pouch and are protruded when feeding.
Habitat Proturans occur worldwide, and are found in moist soil, moss, leaf mold, in decaying wood, and under bark.

■ SPRINGTAILS
Characteristics These pale, wingless insects have elongate or oval bodies. They have a distinctive jumping organ, called a furcula, which helps them "spring" their way out of danger.
Habitat Springtails live in soil and leaf litter, under bark, and in rotting wood. Some species live on the surface of freshwater ponds or along the seashore.

■ DIPLURANS
Characteristics Diplurans are slender, soft-bodied primitive insects with two abdominal

SNAPSHOT

ORDER FEATURES Pale and wingless; diplurans, proturans, and some springtails lack eyes; elongate body; springtails have furcula

DIET Insect and plant matter

LIFE CYCLE Metamorphosis is incomplete; eggs laid in soil

HABITAT Damp, cool conditions, including soil, leaf litter, moss, in fungi, and around ponds

DISTRIBUTION Worldwide

LINKS IN THE CHAIN
Springtails are among the most abundant of all the insect orders. They are vital components of the food chain.

sensory "tails" or cerci. They have long, segmented antennae and biting mouthparts that are contained within a pouch. Eggs are laid in soil and sometimes females guard their brood.

Habitat They live in soil, under rocks, and in rotting vegetation.

SOIL CREEPER
This dipluran is common in Europe and Asia, and is usually found pushing its way through rotting vegetation and soil.

ARCHAEOGNATHA

2 families

Bristletails

Number of species: 350

Length: Up to ½ in (12 mm)

THYSANURA

4 families

Silverfish

Number of species: 370

Length: ¹/₁₆–³/₄ in (2–20 mm)

SNAPSHOT

ORDER FEATURES **Wingless, simple mouthparts, compound eyes**

DIET **Starchy material, including paper, flour, textiles, and glue**

LIFE CYCLE **Develop without obvious metamorphosis; continuous lifetime molting**

HABITAT **Trees, under rocks, in leaf-litter, houses, and nests**

DISTRIBUTION **Worldwide, mainly in warm areas**

■ BRISTLETAILS

Characteristics Bristletails are small, wingless insects, often covered in dark brown or gray scales. In side view, they have a humped-back appearance. They have compound eyes and three ocelli. There are three long tails at the end of the abdomen. Underneath the abdomen are projections called styles, which may help bristletails to move.

Life cycle, diet, and habitat Bristletails molt continuously throughout their lives. There is no change in the insect's shape, and they continue to molt even after they reach sexual maturity. Females lay batches of eggs in small cracks. Bristletails feed on algae, lichen, and other plant material. They live in leaf litter and rotting vegetable matter.

■ SILVERFISH

Characteristics Silverfish are wingless, flat bodied, and sometimes covered in gray or brown scales. They have simple mouthparts and compound eyes, although some species have no

ON THE ROCKS
Bristletails can jump small distances by flicking their abdomen against rocks. Some are common along rocky coasts.

eyes at all. They have three tails projecting from their abdomen.

Life cycle diet, and habitat

Silverfish molt throughout their life, even after they have reached sexual maturity, with no obvious change in shape. Females lay their eggs in crevices. They eat book bindings, flour, and damp cloth. They live in warm areas, under stones, in trees, and in caves. Domestic species are considered pests.

FLAT OUT
A silverfish lacks wings and some species are blind. The flattened body allows it to wriggle into small crevices.

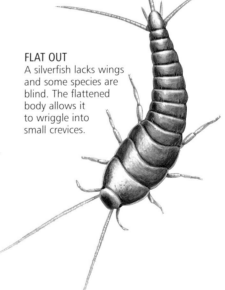

Primitive
Winged Insects

MEMBERS OF THE FOLLOWING ORDERS are admired for their
fragile, jewel-like beauty. They are considered more
primitive than other winged insects (see page 144) because
their delicate, translucent wings cannot be folded back
alongside the body. Short-lived adult mayflies are common
near freshwater ponds and streams; dragonflies and
damselflies are well known for their predatory prowess.
Both orders undergo incomplete metamorphosis and
many species have fascinating life histories.

Mayflies

Number of species: 2,500

Length: $5/32$–$1\,1/4$ in (4–34 mm)

■ CHARACTERISTICS

Mayflies are the only insects that molt after they have functional wings. They have soft bodies, long legs, and two pairs of large, triangular wings that cannot be folded back; instead, the wings are held together above the body when the mayfly is at rest. Adults have vestigial mouthparts and therefore do not feed.

SNAPSHOT

ORDER FEATURES **Usually two pairs of triangular wings, long legs, long abdominal tails**

DIET **Adults do not feed; nymphs eat plants and animals**

LIFE CYCLE **Metamorphosis is incomplete; eggs laid in water**

HABITAT **Near streams, rivers, ponds, and lakes; sometimes near brackish water**

DISTRIBUTION **Worldwide**

■ LIFE CYCLE AND DIET

Mayflies mate in huge swarms, usually at dawn or dusk. Females lay their eggs by dipping their abdomen into the water. They lay between 500 and 3,000 eggs. Metamorphosis is incomplete. Nymphs may go through up to 50 molts and live for up to two years in the nymphal stage. They feed on organic material. When fully grown, they rise to the water's surface and molt into a sub-imago—a form that has the appearance of an adult, but with dull-colored wings. Within one hour or several days, the sub-imago molts into a shiny-winged adult. Adults of some species live for one or two days; others have a life span of only a few hours.

■ HABITAT

Mayflies live near streams, rivers, ponds, and lakes. Some species live near brackish water.

MAY OR MAY NOT

Many mayfly species are becoming rare because pollution levels in rivers and streams are affecting mayfly nymphs.

Damselflies and Dragonflies

Number of species: 5,500

Wingspan: 3/4–63/4 in (20–170 mm)

■ CHARACTERISTICS

Damselflies and dragonflies are the only surviving representatives of the ancient flying insects. They have large compound eyes, three ocelli, biting mouthparts, and short, bristle-like antennae. The long, cylindrical abdomen has short cerci. They have two pairs of large wings with many veins. The forewings and hindwings are roughly the same size. Damselflies have a broad head with eyes widely spaced; dragonflies have a more rounded head and less space between the eyes. Both beat their forewings and hindwings independently during flight. The hindwings beat at a slightly different speed, increasing flight stability. Dragonflies are strong fliers and active hunters. They hunt by forming a basket with their legs to scoop up prey during flight. Damselflies are weaker fliers; they sit and wait for prey to come within reach.

■ LIFE CYCLE AND DIET

Males transfer sperm from a genital opening on the ninth segment of the abdomen to a storage organ on the third segment. During mating, the male clasps the female behind

---

SNAPSHOT

ORDER FEATURES **Large eyes, two pairs of membranous wings**
DIET **Other insects**
LIFE CYCLE **Metamorphosis is incomplete; eggs laid in water and on aquatic plants**
HABITAT **Near water. Aquatic nymphs have abdominal gills**
DISTRIBUTION **Worldwide**
REMARK **Despite common beliefs, dragonflies do not sting**

WINGS TOGETHER
At rest, damselflies hold their wings together above their body; dragonflies tend to hold their wings outstretched.

the head, while the female bends her abdomen to connect to the genitalia of the male. Sperm is transferred into the female's sperm storage organ. Eggs are deposited inside water plants. Members of this order develop by incomplete metamorphosis. The aquatic nymphs have feathery gills projecting from their abdomen. They feed using modified mouthparts that they shoot forward to grasp prey.

■ HABITAT
Most species are found near fast- and slow-flowing water.

SEEING ALL
The huge compound eyes of dragonflies and damselflies allow them incredible precision when hunting, even at dusk.

BLUE HUE
The exquisite blue color of many dragonflies results from tiny, light-refracting granules on the surface of their body.

SEEING RED
Some male dragonflies develop strong colors as a visual signal to females during breeding.

Winged Insects

THIS CHAPTER EXAMINES SOME of the best-known insect orders in the Class Insecta. Although some contain wingless species, or individuals that are wingless at certain life stages, most have two pairs of wings to speed them from place to place. An insect's wings may be small and inconspicuous, or large and exquisitely patterned. Some have transparent wings; the wings of others are covered in millions of light-reflecting scales. The insects on the following pages are among the most diverse and adaptable species on Earth.

Cockroaches

Number of species: 4,000

Length: ⁵/₁₆–4 in (8–100 mm)

■ CHARACTERISTICS
Cockroaches have a tough, leathery covering and a flattened, oval shape. This shape enables them to scuttle into narrow crevices. They have two pairs of wings; the forewings are toughened and the hindwings are large and membranous. Many species have a shield covering the head, called a pronotum. They are usually brown, red–brown, or dark in color. Most have long, slender antennae. Cockroaches are highly sensitive to vibration. They are fast runners, and some exude or spray toxic chemicals to deter predators. The Madagascan hissing cockroach startles prey by pushing air out of its spiracles to create a hissing sound.

■ LIFE CYCLE AND DIET
Both males and females exude pheromones to signal and attract potential mates. Females lay up

PERFECT SCAVENGERS
Although cockroaches will eat any food scraps, they can survive without food for months.

FEEL THE NOISE
Long antennae and sensitive leg spines can detect minute vibrations

to 50 eggs at a time. These are often enclosed within a hardened egg case, which protrudes from the female's abdomen until it is dropped when the eggs are ready to hatch.

Cockroaches eat mainly decaying organic matter, as well as bird and mammal droppings. Pest species will eat anything from bread to shoe polish.

■ HABITAT
Nearly all cockroaches live in tropical climates. Some are common household pests.

RAINFOREST ROACH
This large wood cockroach lives in a Costa Rican rainforest.

SNAPSHOT
ORDER FEATURES Flattened, oval body; head often covered with a pronotum
DIET Decaying organic matter
LIFE CYCLE Metamorphosis is incomplete; eggs in egg case
HABITAT Leaf litter, under bark, in caves; pest species around sewers and in houses
DISTRIBUTION Worldwide, mostly in warm regions

Mantids

Number of species: 2,000

Length: 3/4–6 in (20–150 mm)

CREEPING THREAT
A mantid's shape
and coloration help
to conceal it from
its victim.

■ CHARACTERISTICS
Mantids derive their common
name, "praying mantis," from the
way they hold their front legs
together, as if they were praying.
All mantids have large wings and
a triangular head equipped with
large forward-facing eyes.
Binocular vision means they can
calculate distances with pinpoint
accuracy, enabling them to seize
prey in a split second with their
strong front legs. Unlike other
insects, mantids can turn their
head to look behind their body.

■ LIFE CYCLE AND DIET
Mantids develop by incomplete
metamorphosis. Females lay their
eggs inside a papery case that
they then attach to twigs. Some
species guard their egg case
from predators. Mantids eat a
wide range of prey, including
lizards and frogs. They lie in wait
for their prey, using camouflage
to conceal themselves.

■ HABITAT
They live mainly in warmer
regions, on foliage and flowers.

BIG BODIES
Most female praying mantises (above) are larger than their male counterparts.

SURPRISE ATTACK
Poised to strike, this orchid mantis blends in with its flowery surroundings.

SNAPSHOT

ORDER FEATURES **Triangular, mobile head; large, forward-pointing eyes; front legs modified for catching and subduing prey**
DIET **Wide range of insects, spiders, even lizards and frogs**
LIFE CYCLE **Metamorphosis is incomplete; eggs laid in egg case**
HABITAT **On vegetation**
DISTRIBUTION **Worldwide, especially in tropical regions**

Termites

Number of species: 2,750

Length: $5/32–5/8$ in (4–14 mm)

DEMOLITION SQUAD
Termites work in darkness, eating wood from the inside. The damage is often hidden until the wood begins to collapse.

■ CHARACTERISTICS
Termites are social insects. They live in permanent colonies where individuals are differentiated into distinct castes. Typically, they are soft-bodied, pale in color, wingless, with short antennae, chewing mandibles, and reduced eyes. The king and queen have an oval head and two pairs of long wings. Soldier termites are sterile and have larger heads than worker termites.

■ LIFE CYCLE AND DIET
Termites develop through a process of incomplete metamorphosis. They build nests, ranging in size from small structures in trees to extensive underground constructions. A queen termite may produce thousands of eggs each day. Termites are one of the few insects able to digest cellulose.

■ HABITAT
They live in various habitats, including soil, trees, and timber.

SNAPSHOT

ORDER FEATURES Social insects; pale body, mainly wingless, short antennae; differences between castes
DIET Rotting or dead wood, wood fibers, crops
LIFE CYCLE Metamorphosis is incomplete; eggs laid by queen
HABITAT Tree, mud, and underground nests
DISTRIBUTION Mostly tropical

MUD SPIRES
The structure of a large
termite nest allows
air circulation that can
maintain a virtually
constant
temperature.

HEAD BANGER
Damp-wood termites
bang their heads against
the walls of the nest, sending
warning vibrations to other
members of the colony.

ZORAPTERA
1 family

Zorapterans

Number of species: 29

Length: Less than 3/16 in (5 mm)

GRYLLOBLATTODEA
1 family

Ice insects

Number of species: 25

Length: 1/2–1 1/4 in (12–30 mm)

SNAPSHOT
ORDER FEATURES **Small and wingless; downward-pointing (Zoraptera) or forward-pointing (Grylloblattodea) mouthparts**
DIET **Plant matter, live prey**
LIFE CYCLE **Metamorphosis is incomplete**
HABITAT **Rocks, snow, ice, caves**
DISTRIBUTION **Worldwide, except Australia (Zoraptera); Northern Hemisphere (Grylloblattodea)**

■ ZORAPTERANS
Characteristics Also known as angel insects, the tiny, termite-like adults of this order display two forms. One form is pale, wingless, and has no eyes; the other form is darker in color, has eyes, three ocelli, and two pairs of wings. Both forms have downward-pointing mouthparts, similar in appearance to grasshoppers and crickets.
Life cycle, diet, and habitat Zorapterans undergo incomplete metamorphosis. Eggs are laid in leaf litter or rotting wood. Nymphs differ in appearance, depending on whether they develop into winged or wingless adults. Both adults and nymphs eat small arthropods and fungal threads. They are found in leaf litter, rotting wood, and under tree bark. Zorapterans live worldwide, except Australia.

■ ICE INSECTS
Characteristics These small, wingless, pale brown or gray insects are adapted to alpine conditions. They are also known

as rock crawlers, because they are found under stones and on open ground. Their small head has simple, forward-facing mandibles. The eyes may be quite small or completely absent. Ice insects have slender cerci and thread-like antennae.

Life cycle, diet, and habitat Ice insects undergo incomplete metamorphosis. Eggs are laid in rotten wood, moss, and in soil. It

COOL CUSTOMER
Also known as rock crawlers, ice insects were first discovered in 1906 in the Canadian Rockies. They are often found crawling over snow, ice, and rocks, especially after dark.

may take nymphs more than five years to develop to adulthood. Adults eat plant matter and also hunt for insect prey. They live in the cooler mountainous areas of the Northern Hemisphere.

DERMAPTERA

Earwigs

Number of species: 1,900

Length: 9/32–2 in (7–50 mm)

ADULT AND NYMPH
Earwig nymphs molt up to five times before becoming adults. They increase in size, but essentially look like their parents.

■ CHARACTERISTICS
Earwigs are flattened insects with short forewings that cover and protect the larger, fan-shaped hindwings. The abdomen is segmented and mobile. At the end of the abdomen is a pair of pincer-like cerci. The cerci are usually straight in females and curved in males. They have a mainly defensive function, but they can give a relatively painless pinch. Some earwigs are pests of flowers and fruits. Many species produce foul-smelling chemicals to deter predators.

■ LIFE CYCLE AND DIET
Earwigs develop by incomplete metamorphosis. Most females lay eggs in soil or leaf litter; some give birth to live nymphs. Female earwigs protect their eggs and young by licking them clean and guarding them from predators. They may also feed the hatched nymphs by regurgitating a portion of their own meal.

■ HABITAT
They are found in soil and leaf litter, under bark, and in crevices.

SNAPSHOT

ORDER FEATURES **Flat, elongate body; segmented abdomen bearing pincer-like cerci**
DIET **Plant matter and small insects, such as caterpillars**
LIFE CYCLE **Metamorphosis is incomplete; eggs laid in soil**
HABITAT **Leaf litter, sand, debris, riverbanks, crevices**
DISTRIBUTION **Worldwide, in warmer regions**

FEEL THE PINCH
The pincer-like cerci on the abdomen of male earwigs are curved. They are used in prey capture and may also have a defensive function.

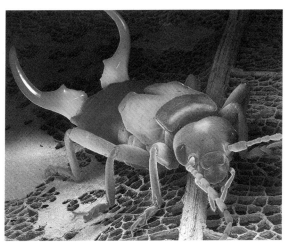

FLOWER POWER
The European earwig is a well-known pest of crops and garden plants, particularly flowers.

Stoneflies

Number of species: 2,000

Length: $3/16-2^{1}/2$ in (5–65 mm)

■ CHARACTERISTICS
Stoneflies are soft-bodied, slender insects that are usually dull brown to dark brown, although some are pale yellow in color. Most have long cerci on the abdomen and all species have two pairs of similar-size transparent wings. When resting, they fold their wings tightly around their body, giving the rounded appearance of a stone. Most stoneflies have simple mouthparts, although some short-lived, non-feeding adults have none at all.

■ LIFE CYCLE AND DIET
Males court females by vibrating the underside of their abdomen on the ground. Females lay masses of eggs in water, sometimes formed into a sticky ball. Most nymphs live an aquatic existence, feeding on algae and detritus. They have two, long filaments on their abdomen. Nymphs may molt 30 times and take up to 5 years to become adults. Adults usually emerge from the water in midwinter or early spring. Many adults are short-lived and do not feed.

■ HABITAT
Most prefer cool climates, and are always found near water.

SNAPSHOT

ORDER FEATURES **Flat, slender bodies, long cerci; dull coloration; transparent wings**
DIET **Plant matter, small insects, such as caterpillars**
LIFE CYCLE **Metamorphosis is incomplete; eggs laid in water**
HABITAT **Near lakes, springs, on vegetation near running water**
DISTRIBUTION **Worldwide, but mostly Northern Hemisphere**

STONE'S THROW
At rest, and usually close to a stream, adult stoneflies roll their transparent wings tightly around their body.

Grasshoppers and Crickets

Number of species: 20,000

Length: 3/16–3 1/4 in (5–85 mm)

■ CHARACTERISTICS

These large and easily recognizable insects include grasshoppers, crickets, mole-crickets, cave crickets, and katydids. They all have chewing mouthparts and highly modified hindlegs for jumping. Most have small, tough forewings covering the larger, membranous hind-wings. Many species "sing" by rubbing pegs on the hindlegs against hard ridges along the wings. These mating songs are used to attract females.

■ LIFE CYCLE AND DIET

All species undergo incomplete metamorphosis. Most lay eggs on the ground, in soil, on bark, or on vegetation. They eat plant and animal matter.

■ HABITAT

Orthopterans are found in a wide range of terrestrial habitats, including deserts, grasslands, forests, caves, and underground.

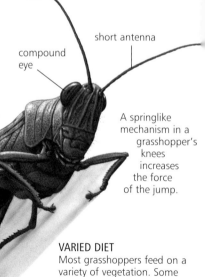

short antenna

compound eye

A springlike mechanism in a grasshopper's knees increases the force of the jump.

muscular hindleg

VARIED DIET
Most grasshoppers feed on a variety of vegetation. Some species are brightly colored.

ORTHOPTERA

ORDER FEATURES Chewing mouthparts; strong hindlegs adapted for jumping
DIET Plant and animal matter
LIFE CYCLE Metamorphosis is incomplete; eggs laid in soil, under bark, or in detritus
HABITAT Grasslands, woodlands, underground, on vegetation
DISTRIBUTION Worldwide, in subtropical and temperate areas

■ GRASSHOPPERS

Characteristics Grasshoppers have relatively short antennae. Females are usually larger than males and they do not have a conspicuous ovipositor. Males sing during the daytime to attract females, who pick up the calls with "ears" (tympanal organs) on their abdomen. Many grasshopper species have camouflage coloration; others produce poisonous chemicals for defensive purposes. Pest species, called locusts, swarm in vast numbers—sometimes comprising several billion individuals— to devastate food crops.

Life cycle Females lay egg masses in the ground, often surrounded by a foamy, protective secretion.

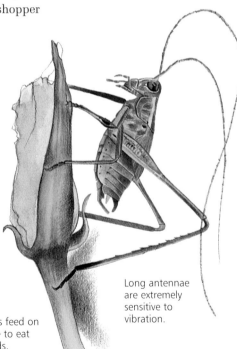

DINING OUT
American tree crickets feed on caterpillars that come to eat evening primrose buds.

Long antennae are extremely sensitive to vibration.

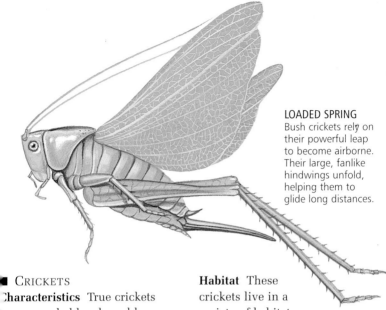

LOADED SPRING
Bush crickets rely on their powerful leap to become airborne. Their large, fanlike hindwings unfold, helping them to glide long distances.

▮ CRICKETS

Characteristics True crickets have rounded heads and long, spindle-like antennae. Most species are black or brown. The female's ovipositor is usually round and shaped like a needle.

Leaf-rolling crickets roll leaves to make a nest, which becomes a hiding place during the day.

Mole-crickets are burrowers, and have front legs adapted for digging. They have short, toughened forewings. The males produce a song that is amplified by their special Y-shaped burrow. Some cricket species are pests on cereal crops.

Habitat These crickets live in a variety of habitats, on vegetation and under the ground.

■ CAVE AND KING CRICKETS

Characteristics Cave crickets are wingless and have very long antennae. Some have soft bodies and reduced eyes. They lay their eggs in sand on the cave floor.

King crickets (also known as Jerusalem crickets or wetas) are large, wingless insects with short antennae. Adults venture out of their burrows after nightfall.

Habitat They live in caves, in rotten wood, and underground.

■ KATYDIDS

Characteristics Katydids (also called bush crickets or long-horned grasshoppers) communicate using sharp clicks and buzzes; only both sexes of the "true" katydids of North America sing "*katy*-DID." Males produce their song by scraping their wings across their hindlegs. Females of some species have a large, sickle-shaped ovipositor. Most katydids are green or brown in color. Their veined, leaf-like front wings, which cover most of their body,

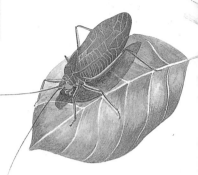

TRUE KATYDID
Male katydids sing the characteristic "katy-did" call often heard on warm summer evenings. Most females are mute, but some respond with a chirp.

provide excellent camouflage. Many species mimic the shape and color of bark and leaves. Some startle enemies by flashing colored hindwings.

Life cycle, diet, and habitat After mating, katydids lay their eggs in soil or inside plants. Nymphs may go through up to six nymphal stages before adulthood. Katydids are mainly found in dense foliage.

KATYDID CONFUSION
Katydids (left) transform themselves by flicking open their colorful, patterned wings to startle predators. Some species, such as this mountain katydid (right), also take on a defensive posture.

Stick Insects and Leaf Insects

Number of species: 2,500

Length: 1–11½ in (25–290 mm)

SNAPSHOT

ORDER FEATURES Stick-like or leaf-like body; mostly nocturnal and slow-moving
DIET Plant matter
LIFE CYCLE Metamorphosis is incomplete; eggs scattered or laid in soil or glued to plants
HABITAT Among the foliage of trees and shrubs
DISTRIBUTION Mainly tropical regions or warm, temperate areas

■ CHARACTERISTICS

Stick insects and leaf insects are mostly nocturnal. They protect themselves from daytime predators by hiding among foliage. Most remain motionless when they are disturbed, holding their legs alongside their body. Others produce smells, noises, or regurgitate food to repel predators. Males are usually smaller than females.

■ LIFE CYCLE AND DIET

Females usually scatter their eggs from the abdomen. Development is via incomplete metamorphosis. Most species eat plant matter.

■ HABITAT

Members of this order are usually found among thick vegetation.

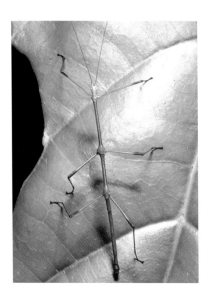

RED-KNEED WALKING STICK
This colorful stick insect lives in the dense foliage of Mount Kinabalu, Borneo. Most stick insects feed on plants at nighttime.

ORANGE FLASH
This orange walking stick displays a flash of its fan-shaped wings. Only the males possess wings.

LOOSE LEGS
Some stick insects shed a leg when seized by a predator. The lost limb usually grows back again.

Webspinners

Number of species: 300

Length: $^1/_8$–$^3/_4$ in (3–20 mm)

■ CHARACTERISTICS
Webspinners are small, soft-bodied, gregarious insects that are not often observed. Their common name reflects the females' ability to make large, protective, silk tunnels in soil, under bark, and in leaf litter.

Webspinners have short legs. They have a swollen segment on their front legs that contains silk glands. The silk is extruded through structures on the underside of the body. The webspinner moves its front feet through the silk and a sheet gradually forms.

Males usually have two pairs of narrow, same-size wings; females are wingless. They have chewing mouthparts and round compound eyes. Females have smaller eyes than males.

Webspinners are nocturnal, living inside their tunnels during the day and coming out at night to feed. Males enter the tunnels only to mate with the females.

■ LIFE CYCLE AND DIET
Webspinners undergo incomplete metamorphosis. Females show a degree of maternal care. They lay small clusters of eggs along the sides of the tunnel, and then cover them with silk and detritus. The female may guard her eggs, licking and moving them. Once hatched, she may feed the nymphs pre-chewed food.

Some individuals congregate in one area, each within their silk

---

SNAPSHOT

ORDER FEATURES Small, elongate body; swollen segment on front legs containing silk glands

DIET Rotting or dead wood, wood fibers, crops

LIFE CYCLE Metamorphosis is incomplete; females show degree of parental care

HABITAT Wide variety, including in bark, tree holes, under stones

DISTRIBUTION Worldwide

tunnel. Females and nymphs
remain with this "colony;" adult
males fly off to other colonies to
mate with females.

Females and nymphs feed on
a variety of vegetation, including
bark, leaf litter, moss, and
lichens. Males are probably
non-feeding and are short-lived.

SILKEN HOME
Webspinners have swollen areas on their
front legs that contain silk glands. This
silk is made into a protective tunnel.

■ HABITAT
Webspinners are found in a
wide variety of habitats, from
deserts to rainforests.

Booklice and Barklice

Number of species: 3,000

Length: $1/64$–$1/4$ in (0.5–6 mm)

Parasitic Lice

Number of species: 6,000

Length: $1/32$–$1/4$ in (1–6 mm)

■ BOOKLICE AND BARKLICE

Characteristics These small, soft-bodied insects have two pairs of membranous wings (if present), a large, bulging forehead, and long, slender antennae. When folded, the wings are held up over the body like a roof.

Life cycle, diet, and habitat Most species lay eggs, although some give birth to live young. Some lay batches of eggs on dead leaves and then cover them with silken threads; others lay their eggs in leaf litter, tree bark, or birds' nests. They develop through incomplete metamorphosis. Nymphs are usually similar to adults. Adults and nymphs feed on lichen, fungi, molds, and pollen. Some are considered pests, particularly those that feed on books. These insects live in dry leaf litter, under bark or stones, in debris, and inside buildings and food stores.

LARGE GATHERING
Barclice are small and usually incon-spicuous, but enormous populations can be found on some trees.

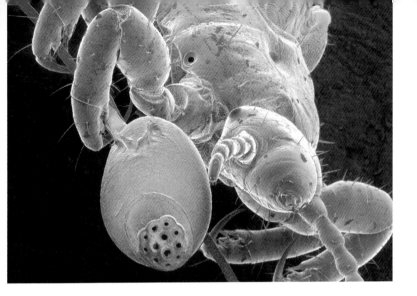

■ PARASITIC LICE

Characteristics Parasitic lice have flattened, wingless bodies. They use their specialized mouthparts for biting skin, fur, or feathers.

Life cycle, diet, and habitat These lice develop through incomplete metamorphosis and are exclusively blood feeders. They live permanently on the exterior of mammals (including humans) and birds. The human body louse lives in clothing and then latches onto the host's body; head lice spend their entire lives in human hair.

HAIR CEMENT
This head louse, magnified 100 times, lays its eggs (nits) singly and then cements each one to the base of a hair.

SNAPSHOT
ORDER FEATURES Wings held rooflike above body (Psocoptera); flattened, wingless (Phthiraptera)
DIET Pollen, paper (Psocoptera); blood, skin (Phthiraptera)
LIFE CYCLE Metamorphosis is incomplete
HABITAT Leaf litter, food stores (Psocoptera); skin, feathers, and fur (Phthiraptera)
DISTRIBUTION Worldwide

Bugs

Number of species: 82,000

Length: 1/32–4 in (1–100 mm)

■ CHARACTERISTICS
Members of this order range in
size from minute, wingless aphids
to giant, frog-catching water bugs.
All possess specialized sucking
and piercing mouthparts,
consisting of a central tube

(rostrum) and four, sharp-tipped
stylets. To feed, a bug pierces the
food source with its stylets and
then pushes its rostrum into the
wound. It pumps in saliva, which
partly digests the food, and then
sucks up the liquid. A bug's front
wings are often leathery at the

WELL SHIELDED
This hawthorn shield bug feeds on ripe
hawthorn berries. Some female shield
bugs guard their eggs until they hatch.

base and clear at the tips. Its transparent hindwings are shorter than its front wings.

This guide covers three of the four suborders of the Hemiptera, representing some of the best-known families in the order.

LIFE CYCLE AND DIET

Most bugs develop by incomplete metamorphosis. Females lay their eggs in soil, under bark, and on vegetation. Some produce live

OFF THE SCENT

Stink bugs produce defensive odors from special glands on the thorax. Their bright colors warn predators to stay away.

young; others reproduce asexually. Most are plant-eaters; some feed on blood and animal fluids.

HABITAT

Bugs live in all terrestrial and aquatic habitats, including the surface of some oceans.

True Bugs

Number of species: 36,000

Length: $^{1}/_{32}$–4 in (1–100 mm)

■ CHARACTERISTICS
True bugs vary widely in shape, size, color, habitat, and diet. All have specialized piercing and sucking mouthparts. They also have long antennae with five or fewer segments.

■ LIFE CYCLE AND DIET
All true bugs undergo incomplete metamorphosis. They usually lay their eggs on or in plants, in soil, on bark, or in cracks or crevices. Only true bugs have species that are blood-feeders and insect predators. Most species

UNDERCOVER BUGS
As their name and appearance imply, bark bugs live on or under bark. They feed on fungus growing on the bark.

suck sap and other plant fluids from vegetation. Many are significant crop pests.

■ HABITAT
The majority of true bugs live on vegetation and many spend winter hibernating in leaf litter or clumps of grass. Some true bugs are exclusively aquatic, while others live in close association with birds and mammals, including humans.

SNAPSHOT

ORDER FEATURES **Piercing and sucking mouthparts (rostrum); tips of forewings transparent**
DIET **Sap, other plant fluids, blood, animal body fluids**
LIFE CYCLE **Metamorphosis is incomplete; eggs laid in soil, on vegetation, under bark**
HABITAT **All terrestrial habitats, freshwater and ocean surface**
DISTRIBUTION **Worldwide**

MOVING INCUBATOR
A female giant water bug glues her eggs onto the back of a male. While carrying the eggs, he is unable to use his wings.

■ SHIELD BUGS

Characteristics Shield bugs (or acanthosomatids) have a distinctive, triangular shield on their thorax, tipped with a pale, Y-shaped mark. Most are green, gray, or brown in color.

Life cycle, diet, and habitat One of the best-known species is the parent bug. Female parent bugs guard their eggs and nymphs under their body. Most shield bugs suck sap from foliage. They live in warm areas, often in woodland and scrubland.

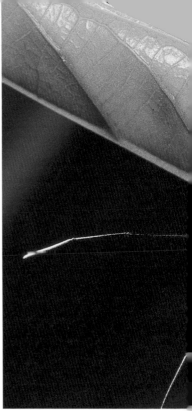

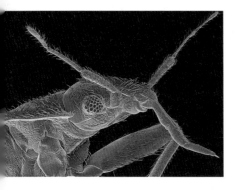

MIDNIGHT SNACK
Bed bugs are nighttime feeders. They pierce their host with their needlelike rostrum and feed on blood.

■ BED BUGS

Characteristics These wingless insects are oval and flattened. They feed by sucking blood from humans, other mammals, and from birds. They can be serious pests, but because of improved hygiene and modern pesticides they are now less common.

Life cycle, diet, and habitat

Bedbugs lay their eggs close to
a host. They have five nymphal
stages; each stage relies on a large
blood meal for its survival. These
nighttime feeders sense their host
by body heat. Although there are
only 90 species, bedbugs are
widely distributed.

FLAG FLYING
The colorful expansions on the hindlegs
of this flag-footed bug may be used to
distract predators.

■ SQUASH BUGS
Characteristics Some species
display bright colors and flag-like
expansions on their hindlegs.

Life cycle, diet, and habitat
Some species of squash bug use squash plants as hosts for their nymphs. They are found in warmer regions, and live on a wide variety of plants. Some species are crop pests.

GLIDING STROKE
Water boatmen use their fringed hindlegs as oars to push them through the water.

■ AQUATIC BUGS
Characteristics Aquatic bugs, such as water boatmen, use their hindlegs like oars to move them across the water. Their forelegs are used for catching prey, while their middle legs are used to grip plants. The long, thin, hair-fringed legs of water striders and ripple bugs enable them to spread their weight evenly on the water without falling through the surface of a pond.

Life cycle, diet, and habitat Most species lay eggs in or on aquatic plants. They live in streams, ponds, marshes, and swamps.

WATER SKATING
The water strider uses surface tension to skate on the water's surface. Hairs on its feet help to repel water, thus keeping it afloat.

BACK STROKE
A backswimmer
swims upside down
underwater. It stores
air bubbles under its
wings, absorbing
oxygen through
its spiracles.

■ STINK BUGS AND ALLIES
Characteristics Stink bugs are a large and well-known group. Many species are very common and abundant. Most can produce strong odors as a defensive measure. Shield-backed bugs are mostly colorful, and often resemble beetles. The middle section of the thorax (scutellum) is large and almost covers the body. Assassin bugs have long, thin hindlegs and strong, short forelegs for grasping prey.

Life cycle, diet, and habitat The majority glue their eggs onto plants. Stink bugs and shield-backed bugs are sap-suckers. Assassin bugs are predators of other insects, stabbing them with their sharp rostrum. All are found on a wide variety of vegetation.

NO JOKE
Jester bugs use their piercing mouthparts to suck nectar. Their mouthparts are tucked away in a groove on the underside of the body when they are not feeding.

QUICK CHANGE
Australian harlequin bugs are bright orange as adults, but may be orange and steely blue as nymphs.

TOUCHÉ!
An assassin bug uses its sharp beak to stab its victim. It then sucks out the insect's body fluids.

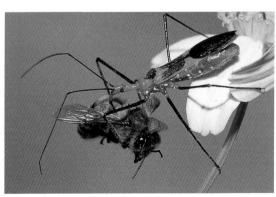

Cicadas and Allies

Number of species: 35,000

Length: 1/8–4 in (3–100 mm)

■ CHARACTERISTICS
Members of families in this
suborder include the froghoppers,
leafhoppers, treehoppers, and the
cicadas. Most species have stout
bodies, broad and blunt heads,
and large, wide eyes. Many
display camouflage or warning
coloration. Some produce mating
calls in special abdominal organs.

■ LIFE CYCLE AND DIET
All cicadas and hoppers develop
by incomplete metamorphosis.
Eggs are laid inside plants or
in soil. Most feed on sap from
plant stems and roots.

■ HABITAT
These bugs are found on a wide
variety of vegetation, including
trees, shrubs, and flowers.

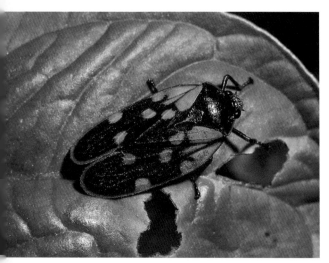

BRIGHT BUGS
Froghoppers (left)
often display
bright warning
colors. They live on
a variety of trees
and shrubs,
particularly in
warm climates.

MATING CALLS
Male cicadas
(right) produce
their loud
mating songs in
abdominal organs.
Males can produce
a number of
different songs.

CUNNING DISGUISE
The peanut bug's shape and dull coloration help to conceal it from hungry birds.

■ FROGHOPPERS
Characteristics Froghoppers are excellent jumpers. They have squat bodies and large, round eyes. Some species are drab brown in color; others display bright red-and-black, or yellow-and-black patterns.
Life cycle, diet, and habitat Froghoppers lay their eggs in soil. The nymphs live under the ground, covered by a frothy, spittle-like mass of bubbles. They live on a wide variety of plants and shrubs, feeding on plant sap.

■ CICADAS
Characteristics Cicadas are more often heard than seen. Only the males produce a song in special organs on their abdomen. Usually green or dark brown in color, they have a wide head and prominent eyes.
Life cycle, diet, and habitat Females lay eggs inside slits that they cut in trees and shrubs. The hatchlings drop onto the ground and burrow into the soil. The nymphs then emerge, crawling up trees before their final molt

into adulthood. Some species have a life cycle of 13 to 17 years.

■ FULGORIDS

Characteristics Many fulgorids, including the bizarre peanut bug, have strangely shaped heads. They remain camouflaged in their surroundings until disturbed, suddenly flashing the eyespots or bright colors on their wings.

Life cycle, diet, and habitat Fulgorids surround their eggs with a protective secretion. They live in tropical and subtropical regions and feed on plant sap.

LIVING THORNS
Treehoppers, or thorn bugs, feed in clusters, sucking up plant sap. Their spiny shape deters birds from eating them, but also provides them with an extremely effective disguise.

■ LEAF- AND TREEHOPPERS

Characteristics Leafhoppers have triangular heads and slim bodies. Treehoppers can be distinguished from leafhoppers by their dome- or thorn-shaped pronotum.

Life cycle, diet, and habitat These bugs lay their eggs inside plant tissue. They live on foliage and feed on plant fluids.

Aphids and Allies

Number of species: 11,000

Length: $^1/_{32}$–$1^1/_2$ in (1–30 mm)

■ CHARACTERISTICS
Aphids, scale insects, and whiteflies belong to different families within the suborder Sternorrhyncha. Aphids are tiny, soft-bodied bugs, with short tubes on their abdomen, called cornicles, capable of making substances to deter predators. Scale insects are usually flat, wingless females that form a protective, scalelike covering over their bodies. Whiteflies look similar to small, white moths and have a powdery substance coating their wings.

■ LIFE CYCLE AND DIET
Aphids reproduce both sexually and asexually. Winged females fly to host plants and then reproduce by a process—parthenogenesis—whereby eggs develop without fertilization, with females giving birth to live nymphs. Like aphids, scale insects have sexual and asexual reproduction, and are able to build up enormous colonies in a very short time. Adult whiteflies lay their eggs on the undersides of leaves. Aphids, scale insects, and whiteflies are significant plant pests.

LIVE BIRTH
Female aphids produce billions of offspring without mating. Here, wingless adult females are giving birth to nymphs.

■ HABITAT
These bugs are found on a wide variety of plants. Scale insects and whiteflies live in warm areas; aphids tolerate cooler climates.

THYSANOPTERA
8 families

Thrips

Number of species: 5,000

Length: $1/32$–$1/2$ in (0.7–12 mm)

■ CHARACTERISTICS
Thrips are slender, black or pale-yellow insects with short antennae and large compound eyes. They have two pairs of narrow wings, fringed with long hairs. They are weak fliers. Their distinctive sucking mouthparts are asymmetrical; one mandible is small and the other is slender and needle-shaped.

FAMILY GROUPS
Adult and nymph tube-tailed thrips feed alongside each other. Some species eat fungi, while others feed on plants or rotting wood.

SNAPSHOT

ORDER FEATURES Slender bodies; two pairs of fringed wings; asymmetrical mouthparts
DIET Sap, pollen, other insects
LIFE CYCLE Neither incomplete nor complete metamorphosis; fertilized eggs produce females, unfertilized eggs produce males
HABITAT On foliage and flowers; some live in soil
DISTRIBUTION Worldwide

■ LIFE CYCLE AND DIET
Thrips undergo a similar reproductive pattern to the Hymenoptera (bees, wasps, and ants), whereby unfertilized eggs produce males and fertilized eggs produce females. Females lay their eggs inside plant tissue. Most thrips feed on plant sap. Banded thrips, however, feed on small insects or pollen grains.

■ HABITAT
Thrips are commonly found on a variety of vegetation. Many species are major crop pests.

Alderflies and Dobsonflies

Number of species: 300

Length: 3/8–3 in (10–75 mm)

■ CHARACTERISTICS
Members of this order have soft bodies, two pairs of similar-size wings, and are weak fliers. At rest, they hold their folded wings in a "roof" over the body.

■ LIFE CYCLE AND DIET
Alderflies and dobsonflies are considered the most primitive insects to develop by complete metamorphosis. Larvae pupate inside a chamber made from moss, sand, or soil. Although adults have large mandibles, they do not feed. The aquatic larvae have gills on their abdomen, and feed on small, water-dwelling insects.

■ DOBSONFLIES
Characteristics Dobsonflies' wings are either clear, or gray or brown in areas. Males have very large mandibles.
Life cycle, diet, and habitat Dobsonflies lay their eggs near water. The aquatic larvae eat small aquatic animals and may take years to develop to adulthood. They occur in temperate regions, and are most often found near running water.

■ ALDERFLIES
Characteristics Smaller than dobsonflies, alderflies have dark-veined wings and no ocelli.

FIGHTING CHANCE
Male dobsonflies have huge mandibles, which are thought to be used in combat with other males, or to hold the female.

LONG DROP
Female alderflies lay their large masses of eggs near water. As they hatch, the larvae drop into the water below.

Life cycle, diet, and habitat
Females lay their egg masses near water. The hatched larvae take up to one year to mature, and feed on small pond life. Adults are often found resting on plants near slow-moving water.

Snakeflies

Number of species: 150

Length: 1/4–1 1/4 in (6–30 mm)

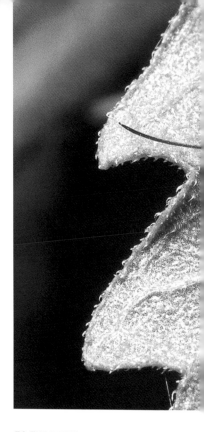

■ CHARACTERISTICS
Snakeflies are dark in color,
with two pairs of similar-size
wings and a distinctive "neck,"
consisting of a long pronotum
and a shiny, flat head. The head
can be raised and lowered on the
pronotum. Snakeflies get their
name from the snakelike way in
which they hold their prey. They
move their head up and forward
to strike at their victim. They
have forward-pointing, chewing
mouthparts. Female snakeflies
are larger than males.

■ LIFE CYCLE AND DIET
These insects develop by
complete metamorphosis.
Females lay several hundred
eggs through a slender ovipositor,
usually under bark or in rotting
wood. The strong-limbed larvae
forage for food under loose tree
bark, in rotten trees, and in leaf

TO THE POINT
Female snakeflies are usually larger than
males. They have a long, slender
ovipositor to lay eggs in tree bark.

litter. Unlike the larvae of the
closely related alderflies (Order
Megaloptera), snakefly larvae are
land-dwellers and do not possess

gills. Adults and larvae are predators, both feeding on other soft-bodied insects and larvae, but they may also scavenge for food.

■ HABITAT
Most snakefly species live in the Northern Hemisphere, in wooded areas among lush vegetation.

SNAPSHOT

ORDER FEATURES Snakelike head and neck; two pairs of clear, similar-size wings

DIET Other soft-bodied insects and insect larvae

LIFE CYCLE Metamorphosis is complete; eggs laid under bark; larvae are terrestrial

HABITAT On vegetation, in bark

DISTRIBUTION Mostly Northern Hemisphere

Net-veined Insects

Number of species: 4,000

Wingspan: 1/4–4³/4 in (6–120 mm)

■ CHARACTERISTICS
Most members of this order have large compound eyes and long antennae. The two pairs of wings are of similar size and are held over the body like a roof when the insect is at rest. The major wing veins are "netted" or forked.

■ LIFE CYCLE AND DIET
All species develop by complete metamorphosis. Most are active hunters of flying insects. Some eat aphids, mites, and thrips; others eat nectar or pollen.

■ HABITAT
Most live on vegetation— usually near water—in tropical, temperate, or semi-arid regions.

■ LACEWINGS AND OWLFLIES
Characteristics Lacewings are usually green in color, with large

WISE OWLS
Owlflies can be identified by their long antennae with clubbed ends. They are skilled nocturnal predators, deftly seizing insect prey on the wing.

gold or red eyes. Adults are
attracted toward lights shining
from houses. Owlflies have
distinctive, clubbed antennae
and patterned wings. Adults
seize prey in the air.
Life cycle, diet, and habitat Both
insects lay eggs on vegetation;
lacewing eggs are laid on stalks
and owlflies lay eggs in spirals.
Both eat insects and live on
vegetation in dry habitats.

LION HEART
Antlions resemble damselflies, but can
be distinguished by their conspicuous,
knobbed antennae.

■ ANTLIONS
Characteristics Antlions have
clubbed antennae and large eyes.
Life cycle, diet, and habitat Their
eggs are laid in soil. The larvae
construct pits to trap insect prey.
Most live in warm, dry areas.

Beetles

Number of species: 370,000

Length: $^1/_{32}$–$7^1/_2$ in (1–190 mm)

BREAK OUT
Weevils have sharp, chewing mouthparts. Most feed by boring into grain.

■ CHARACTERISTICS

The Order Coleoptera is the largest in the animal kingdom. In fact, almost one in every four animals on Earth is a beetle. Arguably the most successful insects, beetles have colonized every terrestrial and aquatic habitat. They vary enormously in size, ranging from the minute feather-winged beetle, only just visible to the naked eye, to the male hercules beetle from Central America, which can be more than $7^1/_2$ inches (19 cm) long.

HEAD-TAPPER
The deathwatch beetle's head-tapping mating signals were often heard in quiet rooms during a funeral wake.

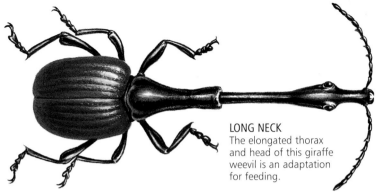

LONG NECK
The elongated thorax and head of this giraffe weevil is an adaptation for feeding.

Despite this amazing variation in color and shape, beetles have one important feature in common—all have hardened forewings, called elytra, that protect the delicate, membranous hindwings folded underneath. In all species, the elytra meet down the middle of the body. A beetle's elytra protect its spiracles and fragile hindwings from being damaged as it clambers around in search of food. Aquatic insects use the space under their elytra to store air for breathing. Most beetles have large compound eyes and antennae composed of ten or more segments.

This guide covers a selection of representative families within this huge order, from wood-borers to flesh-eaters.

HIDDEN JEWELS
Many weevils have bright patterns and colors, produced by light reflecting off microscopic hairs, and by the structure of their body case.

■ LIFE CYCLE AND DIET
Beetles undergo complete metamorphosis. The male usually clings to the female's back during mating. She then lays eggs on or inside suitable vegetation, on soil or bark, inside wood or dung, in leaf litter or fungi, or near a host insect. Some beetle species have

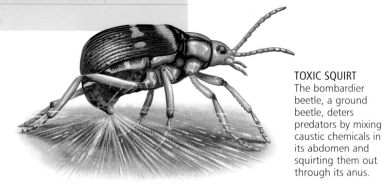

TOXIC SQUIRT
The bombardier beetle, a ground beetle, deters predators by mixing caustic chemicals in its abdomen and squirting them out through its anus.

lengthy larval stages. Most beetle species are plant-eaters, and will consume anything from hardwood to nectar. Carpet beetles feed not only on rugs but also on stored grain, upholstery, fur, and stuffed toys. Some, such as tiger beetles, are predators of other insects; specialized parasitic species are also known. Many beetles are significant crop and timber pests.

■ HABITAT
Beetles are found in all habitats, from rainforests and streams to deserts and caves. Some rove beetles live only in the fur of beavers; others live on birds or in the nests of bees. Some clerid beetles live in termite nests, or on carrion. Many beetles make their home in damp leaf litter.

■ WOOD-BORING BEETLES
Characteristics These small beetles are elongate to oval. The best-known species are the furniture beetle and the common wood-borer. They can fit their short legs into special grooves on the underside of the body.
Life cycle, diet, and habitat The eggs are laid on a food source, usually dry wood. The larvae bore circular tunnels as they eat through the wood. They are able to digest the fibers with the assistance of yeasts found within their gut. Wood-borers live in wooded areas, warehouses and inside buildings.

DAPPER UNIFORMS
Soldier beetles get their common name from their yellow-and-black coloring, similar to military uniforms.

VIOLIN BEETLE
With its flattened elytra and semi-transparent "wings," this ground beetle squeezes between bracket fungi.

LONG HORNS
This longhorn beetle has extremely long antennae, typical of family members.

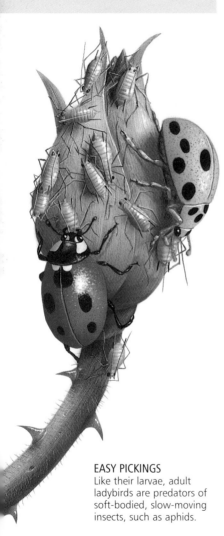

EASY PICKINGS
Like their larvae, adult ladybirds are predators of soft-bodied, slow-moving insects, such as aphids.

■ JEWEL, SOLDIER, AND GROUND BEETLES

Characteristics Most jewel beetles are metallic green, red, or blue, with large eyes and short antennae. Soldier beetles have distinctive, curved jaws, long, thin antennae, and are usually red and black, or yellow and black. Ground beetles are long and flattened, sometimes with a metallic sheen. A few produce caustic substances, which they blast out from the end of their abdomen, to deter predators.

Life cycle, diet, and habitat Some jewel beetles have heat-detecting organs at the base of their legs, used to seek out their preferred egg-laying sites in burned forests. They lay their eggs in wood. When the larvae hatch, they chew tunnels through dead trees. Adults eat flowers, nectar, and pollen. Soldier beetles scatter their eggs on the ground. Both the adults and larvae are predators. Ground beetles lay their eggs on soil or vegetation. The larvae and adults are primarily predacious.

POLLEN FEAST
Some checkered beetles (above) are pollen-feeders. They are found mainly in tropical areas.

GRUB UP
The grub of the seven-spot ladybird (below) needs strong legs to climb after the aphids that it feeds on.

EGG CLUSTERS
Female ladybirds (left) lay egg clusters on foliage. After about one week, the first larvae begin to emerge from the eggs.

CLICK BEETLE
A click beetle escapes danger by lying on its back and keeping still. It suddenly snaps upward, hurling itself out of harm's way.

■ LADYBIRDS AND
  CHECKERED BEETLES
Characteristics Ladybirds are mostly brightly colored, often with black spots or stripes. They are round-bodied and have short legs. Checkered beetles have a flat, elongate shape. They are often covered with long hairs and some have clubbed antennae.
Life cycle, diet, and habitat
Ladybirds glue single eggs or egg clusters to plants. Both adults and larvae eat soft-bodied insects. They are sometimes used as biological controls on insect pests. Checkered beetles lay their eggs in rotting wood. Larvae feed on the larvae of other insects.

■ CLICK BEETLES
Characteristics These elongate beetles are mostly dull in color. Some have distinctive markings on the thorax. Click beetles can propel themselves into the air, producing a loud, clicking sound that deters predators.
Life cycle, diet, and habitat Click beetles lay eggs in soil, with their larvae taking a year to develop. The larvae of some species are called wireworms, and may cause damage to potato crops.

■ DIVING BEETLES
Characteristics Diving beetles have many adaptations for aquatic life, including a smooth

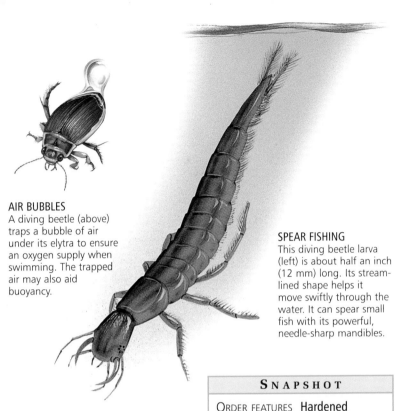

AIR BUBBLES
A diving beetle (above) traps a bubble of air under its elytra to ensure an oxygen supply when swimming. The trapped air may also aid buoyancy.

SPEAR FISHING
This diving beetle larva (left) is about half an inch (12 mm) long. Its streamlined shape helps it move swiftly through the water. It can spear small fish with its powerful, needle-sharp mandibles.

body and fringed hindlegs to help propel them through the water.
Life cycle, diet, and habitat
Female diving beetles lay eggs inside aquatic plants. The larvae pupate in wet soil. Adults and larvae are fierce predators, eating insects, frogs, and small fish.

SNAPSHOT
ORDER FEATURES **Hardened forewings (elytra) that meet down the middle of the body**
DIET **Most eat plant matter; some are predators and scavengers; a few are parasitic**
LIFE CYCLE **Metamorphosis is complete; eggs laid in terrestrial and aquatic habitats**
HABITAT **All habitats**
DISTRIBUTION **Worldwide**

■ FIREFLIES

Characteristics These small, flat beetles are also called lightning bugs. The adults of many species communicate using flashes of green light produced in luminous organs on the abdomen. Males have fully developed wings; some females are wingless.

Life cycle, diet, and habitat Fireflies lay their eggs on vegetation. The larvae are known as glow-worms. They feed on invertebrates and live on plants.

AERIAL ILLUMINATION
Male fireflies flash coded signals to the wingless females on the ground. Females sometimes signal closely related species, luring them and then attacking and eating them.

SEEING THE LIGHT

Fireflies recognize their own species, usually by signaling at specific times of day. Some always signal at dusk for about half an hour; others signal after sunset for several hours.

CARDINAL FLIGHT
As this cardinal beetle takes to the air, it displays the functional use of its elytra as stabilizers during flight.

■ STAG AND FIRE-COLORED
   BEETLES

Characteristics Stag beetles have large, shiny bodies. Males are always larger than females and have huge mandibles equipped with prominent "teeth." These mandibles are used in courtship combat for mating rights. They are designed to clip over a rival beetle and assist in flipping it over during conflict. The best-known fire-colored beetles are the cardinals. They have black, red, or yellow coloring, flat bodies, and serrations on their antennae.
Life cycle, diet, and habitat Female stag beetles lay eggs in rotting tree stumps. Larvae pupate inside cells composed of chewed wood fibers. Adults are sometimes non-feeding or they feed on plant juices. Fire-colored beetles lay eggs under bark. They feed on other insects.

■ BLISTER BEETLES

Characteristics These beetles produce an oily fluid that may cause human skin to blister. They secrete the fluid from their

LONG DEVELOPMENT
Stag beetle larvae take several years to reach adulthood (below). Eggs are laid on rotting wood and the nymphs pupate inside a cell made from wood fibers.

JOUSTING JAWS
The ferocious-looking jaws of male stag beetles (above) are used for grappling with other males for mating rights.

Egg

Larva

Nymph

Adult

leg joints as a deterrent to predators. Many species are soft and leathery; most have red or yellow markings.

Life cycle, diet, and habitat Females lay their eggs in soil. The larvae of some species hide among flowers and grab on to visiting bees. The bees then carry them back to their nest, where they eat the bee's eggs. Adults feed on plant matter. They live mainly on flowers and foliage.

■ SCARAB BEETLES
Characteristics This large family contains more than 16,000 species, and displays a wide variety of shapes, colors, and sizes. All species have distinctive antennae that end in a club shape, and consist of several movable parts. The males of many species have horns, which they use in courtship battles over females. Scarab beetles were important religious symbols in

ON A ROLL
A male and female dung beetle fashion animal droppings into a ball, before the female lays one or more eggs inside it.

SCENT SENSE
Cockchafers, a type of scarab beetle, are nocturnal. Their fanlike antennae, which they spread out when flying, are used to detect scents and wind direction.

Ancient Egypt. Many of the brightly colored species are under threat from over-collection, especially in Central America.

Life cycle, diet, and habitat
Females lay eggs in soil, decaying wood or animal remains, and in the dung of plant-eating mammals. Some roll dung into balls before burying it and laying eggs inside. Some species stay in a nest with the dung balls until the young emerge. Both adults

and larvae eat the moist fungi and yeast in dung. They are usually found on decaying matter, on dung, under bark, or in ant nests.

■ WEEVILS
Characteristics Weevils form the largest family in the animal kingdom. These beetles have a long rostrum, equipped with sharp mouthparts at its tip. Most have camouflage coloring, but some are brightly patterned.

SWEET FOOD
Rose cockchafers, also known as
May beetles, are frequent visitors
to gardens across southern Europe.
They feed on nectar and pollen.

Life cycle, diet, and habitat

Weevils drill a hole in a plant
using their rostrum and then lay
their eggs inside. The larvae are
grub-like. Many adults and larvae
are pests of cereal crops, cotton,
and timber.

BAD SMELL
Adult carrion beetles and their larvae are scavengers. They are attracted to decaying flesh by its odor.

TAIL UP
Some species of rove beetle curve their abdomen into a scorpion-like posture.

■ CARRION BEETLES
AND ROVE BEETLES
Characteristics Carrion beetles are usually flat and soft-bodied, with yellow, orange, or red markings. They have short elytra, exposing some of their segmented abdomen. All rove beetles have short elytra and an exposed, mobile abdomen. Many species have a covering of black and yellow hairs.

Life cycle, diet, and habitat
Carrion beetles lay eggs in the corpses of small mammals that they first bury. They eat rotting plant and animal material. Rove beetles lay their eggs in leaf litter, soil, or fungi. Larvae and adults usually live in the same area. Both eat insects or invertebrates. Some species live in decaying plants, in ant colonies, or on the fur of some mammals.

8 families

Twisted-winged Parasites

Number of species: 560

Length: $^1/_{64}$–$^5/_{32}$ in (0.5–4 mm)

9 families

Scorpionflies and Allies

Number of species: 550

Length: $^1/_{16}$–$1^1/_2$ in (2–40 mm)

■ TWISTED-WINGED PARASITES
Characteristics As the common name suggests, the hindwings of these males have a twisted appearance. Females are wingless and legless, and usually live inside the bodies of other insects as a parasite. They mostly favor bees, wasps, and bugs as hosts.
Life cycle, diet, and habitat Males and females communicate using pheromones. The male mates with the female while she is inside the host's body. The eggs hatch inside the female and the legged larvae emerge and move on to new hosts.

■ SCORPIONFLIES
Characteristics These insects have long and slender bodies, with two pairs of narrow wings. In some species, the males have an upturned abdomen with enlarged genitalia, resembling

WEB RAIDER
Some scorpionfly males appropriate insects captured in spiders' webs, and then present them as a gift to a potential mate.

a scorpion's tail. The head is
lengthened downward to form
a beak-like rostrum.

Life cycle, diet, and habitat
Males sometimes present females
with a gift of food before mating.
Females may refuse males that
offer small or inferior gifts.
Scorpionflies undergo complete
metamorphosis. They lay their
eggs in soil and the larvae usually
pupate under the ground. Most
scorpionflies eat insects, fruit,
nectar, and mosses. Some species,
called hangingflies, dangle from
vegetation, catching passing
insects with their hindlegs.

HANGING AROUND
These scorpionflies, called hangingflies,
mate at night. Males often present
courtship gifts of food to females.

S N A P S H O T
ORDER FEATURES **Females are endoparasites (Strepsiptera); upturned abdomen (Mecoptera)**
DIET **Females eat host's body fluids (Strepsiptera); insects and nectar (Mecoptera)**
LIFE CYCLE **Metamorphosis is complete**
HABITAT **Endoparasitic females (Strepsiptera); among vegetation (Mecoptera)**

SIPHONAPTERA

18 families

Fleas

Number of species: 2,000

Length: 1/32–5/16 in (1–8 mm)

■ CHARACTERISTICS

Fleas are wingless, laterally flattened insects, with tough, shiny bodies covered in bristles. Their mouthparts are modified for sucking blood. Adult fleas are sensitive to heat. They use their small antennae to sense the body heat of a passing mammal or the presence of a mammal's exhaled carbon dioxide. Fleas have a unique mechanism for moving from host to host. Before a jump, muscles squeeze protein pads in the thorax. When the pads are released, they spring back into shape and catapult the flea into the air. Many species are disease spreaders; rodent fleas carried the bacterium that caused bubonic plague in Europe in the 1300s.

■ LIFE CYCLE AND DIET

Fleas undergo complete metamorphosis. Females leave

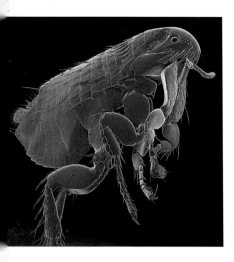

HAIR-RAISING
A flea's body is flattened laterally, making for easier movement between the hairs or feathers of its host.

their host to lay sticky eggs in a host's nest or burrow. Pupation takes place inside a cocoon, which is sometimes composed of silk. The pupae remain in their cocoon until a potential host is nearby. Adult fleas suck blood from their hosts, although they can survive long periods without a meal. The larvae are scavengers, feeding on the host's dried blood, the excrement of the adult fleas, and other detritus.

UNWANTED GUEST
Heavy infestations of fleas may cause the serious illness of a host, in this case a small bird called a house martin.

■ HABITAT
Fleas are ectoparasites. They live on the outside of hosts—usually mammals, but sometimes birds—and feed on them without causing death. Some species feed on a large number of host species (up to 30 in some cases).

DIPTERA

160 families

Flies

Number of species: 122,000

Length: 1/32–2³/4 in (1–70 mm)

■ CHARACTERISTICS

Flies belong to the fourth-largest order of insects. They are characterized by having only one pair of wings. The hindwings are reduced to small, knob-shaped organs called halteres. The halteres vibrate at high speed during flight to keep the fly's body balanced and level. All flies are similar in basic shape. They

WELCOME BREATH
Some non-biting midges have hemoglobin in their blood, which may assist them to carry the oxygen required to survive in stagnant water.

range in size from tiny midges to the Trinidad horse fly, which is the size of a walnut. Most flies have a large head, large compound eyes, and excellent vision. All eat liquid food. They have mouthparts that act like straws or sponges to suck or mop up food. Each foot has hairy pads that secrete oily fluids, enabling flies to stick to glass and ceilings. Because of their dietary habits, many species transmit a variety of bacteria and parasites.

SNAPSHOT

ORDER FEATURES **Two pairs of wings, hindwings modified into halteres; sucking mouthparts**
DIET **Adults take fluids; larvae take fruit, flesh, dung, vegetation**
LIFE CYCLE **Metamorphosis is complete; eggs laid in soil, plants, water, carrion, dung**
HABITAT **A wide range of terrestrial and aquatic habitats**
DISTRIBUTION **Worldwide**

■ LIFE CYCLE AND DIET
Most members of this order undergo complete metamorphosis, transforming

from blind, legless maggots to winged adults. Females lay eggs in soil, under bark, in rotting fruit, inside a host insect, or in flesh or dung. Larvae eat a wide variety of food.

■ HABITAT
Flies are found in virtually all habitats, from aquatic to alpine,

MIDGE ON THE MOVE
Biting midges suck fluids from larger insects or vertebrates. Adults never stray far from their preferred marshy areas.

and from cave to desert. Some species are parasitic; others play an important role in the detritus cycle. Many pest species are found near raw or cooked food.

■ MIDGES

Characteristics Biting midges may be slender or rounded, with a rounded head and feathery antennae. Their bites can cause severe irritation to the skin of humans and other mammals. Non-biting midges can be delicate or stocky. They look very similar to mosquitoes, but do not possess functional mouthparts.

Life cycle, diet, and habitat Male and female biting midges mate in large swarms. Their eggs are laid in damp soil, water, and rotting organic matter. Non-biting midges lay their eggs in a sticky jelly, and deposit them onto aquatic vegetation. Some remain in the larval stage for up to three years; adults live for only a few weeks. Midges are common by ponds, bogs, and near the seashore.

■ MOSQUITOES

Characteristics Some tropical mosquitoes are brightly colored; most are gray, white, and brown. They have long, narrow wings and long, slender, piercing mouthparts. Females are carriers of organisms that cause serious diseases, such as malaria, dengue fever, and encephalitis.

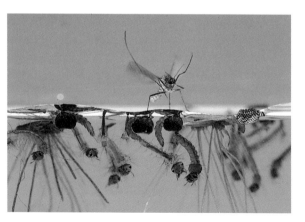

ON THE SURFACE
Mosquitoes lay their eggs on the surface of puddles or stagnant ponds. The writhing larvae breathe from a siphon on their abdomen. Tiny brushes on their head sweep food particles into the mouth.

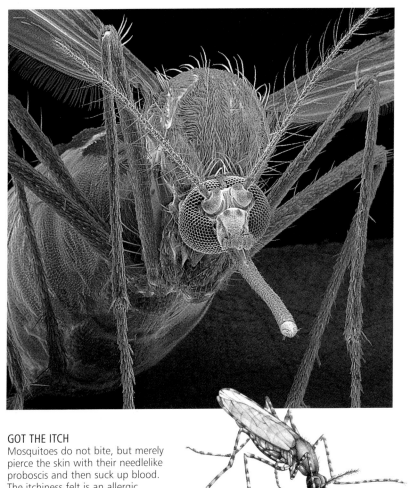

GOT THE ITCH

Mosquitoes do not bite, but merely pierce the skin with their needlelike proboscis and then suck up blood. The itchiness felt is an allergic reaction to the anti-coagulant chemicals the mosquito injects to make the blood flow more freely.

FRAGILE FLIERS
Craneflies are often mistaken for mosquitoes, but they do not bite or suck blood. Instead, these fragile, short-lived flies feed on nectar.

Life cycle, diet, and habitat The life cycle of a mosquito lasts less than three weeks. Females lay eggs on the water's surface, in groups of up to 300 or singly. The larvae eat other mosquito larvae. Adult females feed on the blood of vertebrates; males drink nectar and plant fluids. They live in mainly warm areas, and are found near fresh water, from roadside puddles to mountain lakes.

■ CRANEFLIES
Characteristics Most are gray, black, or brown, with very long legs that they shed if captured.
Life cycle, diet, and habitat Eggs are usually laid in soil. The larvae eat fungi, mosses, and decaying vegetable matter. Many adults feed on nectar. They typically fly at twilight and are short-lived. They are most often found near water or among damp vegetation.

■ BLOWFLIES
Characteristics Blowflies are stout-bodied and bright metallic green or blue. Males and females can be different colors. This group includes the well-known bluebottle and greenbottle flies.

Life cycle, diet, and habitat
Female blowflies lay their eggs—hundreds in a lifetime— in carrion, flesh, and dung. Some species lay larvae instead of eggs. They are found around carcasses, on vegetation, and are also attracted to raw and cooked meat. Some carry diseases, and may lay their eggs on livestock and humans. Because they burrow into flesh, blowfly maggots have been used to remove necrotic tissue after surgery.

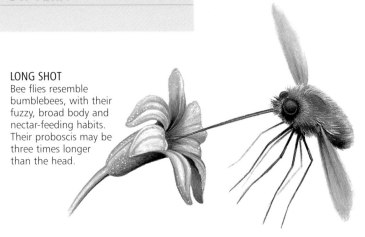

LONG SHOT
Bee flies resemble bumblebees, with their fuzzy, broad body and nectar-feeding habits. Their proboscis may be three times longer than the head.

■ BEE FLIES

Characteristics Some bee fly species are small, but most have broad and furry bodies. They have brown, yellow, or red coloration, and some have bright markings.

Life cycle, diet, and habitat Bee flies are often seen at rest, wings outstretched, on flowers. Some species are important pollinators. The larvae of most species parasitize the larvae of other insects, particularly bees, grasshoppers, and beetles. Females lay their eggs close to the hosts' nests. Adults eat nectar. They are found around flowers or resting on the ground.

■ ROBBER FLIES

Characteristics Robber flies are the most active predators in this order. They are large and beelike, with bulging eyes that give the top of their head a concave appearance. Most species have long facial and body hair, a thick, stout proboscis, and well-developed, spiny bristles on their legs. These bristles assist in the capture of prey. When hunting, robber flies can quickly accelerate from 0 to 25 miles per hour (40 km/h) to snatch a bee or other flying insect in midair. They do not chase prey, but intercept it by darting out from a perch—usually a leaf or a twig.

Life cycle, diet, and habitat Eggs are laid inside plants or in soil. Looking like minute, flattened worms, the larvae eat the eggs and larvae of other insects as they move through soil and leaf litter. Adult robber flies use their sharp proboscis to stab insect prey, usually in the neck. They inject the prey with paralyzing saliva,

MIDAIR ATTACK
A robber fly can suck its victim completely dry within a matter of seconds. Its legs are covered with bristles, some of which are used to hold on to captured prey.

and then suck up the victim's body fluids. Robber flies are found in a variety of habitats, mostly in dry areas.

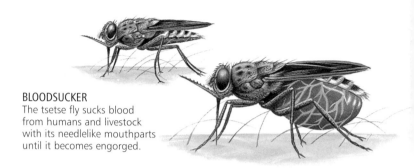

BLOODSUCKER
The tsetse fly sucks blood
from humans and livestock
with its needlelike mouthparts
until it becomes engorged.

■ TSETSE FLIES

Characteristics Tsetse flies are
gray or brown in color, with
needlelike mouthparts used for
sucking up animal and human
blood. Some species transmit the
trypanosome parasite that causes
sleeping sickness, a disease that
makes humans so exhausted they
can barely move. The parasite
does not affect wild animals, but
can be debilitating to livestock.

Life cycle, diet, and habitat
Females lay single eggs, and the
larvae hatch inside the mother's
body, feeding on her secretions.
When a larva emerges from the
female's body, it immediately
pupates. These flies live in open
forests and savanna in Africa.

■ STALK-EYED FLIES

Characteristics These unusual
flies have eyes and tiny antennae
on the tips of long stalks
extending from their head.
Females of some species
sometimes lack eye stalks.

Life cycle, diet, and habitat
When males meet, they compare
eyes; the male with the longest
stalks wins the right to mate with
the female. Stalk-eyed flies stick
their eggs on foliage or on rotting
plant matter. The larvae are
tapered at both ends of the body
and often bore into the stems of
grasses. These flies are found near
vegetation or close to running
water in tropical regions of
Africa and Southeast Asia.

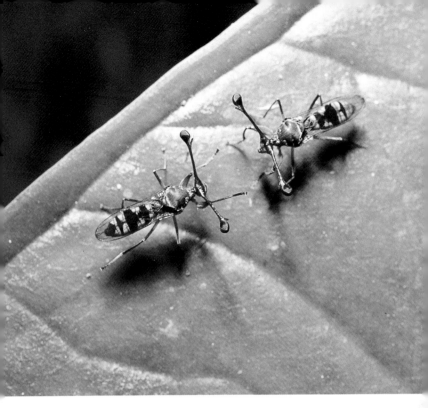

EYES WIDE OPEN
Male stalk-eyed flies from Southeast Asia use their strange eye stalks to threaten rivals and measure their size. The largest male gets to mate.

FRUIT FEEDER
Vinegar flies—both maggots and adults— favor rotting fruit. They sponge up the liquid with their proboscis.

■ HOUSE FLIES

Characteristics Most house flies are dull in color, with dark bristles and long legs.

Life cycle, diet, and habitat Females lay masses of eggs in feces, decomposing matter, on plants, or in birds' nests. The larvae are fast growing and can pupate in a week. Adults lap up anything organic, including dung, with their sponge-like mouth parts. They are found on excrement and decaying matter. House flies spread diseases, including cholera, typhoid, and dysentery.

■ VINEGAR FLIES

Characteristics These flies are also known as pomace flies. They are black, yellow, or brown flies with bright red eyes. Their body may also bear stripes or spots. The best-known species, *Drosophila melanogaster,* is used in genetic studies because of its fast breeding rate and large chromosomes.

Life cycle, diet, and habitat They lay their eggs on or near their food source, including rotting vegetation and fermenting fruit.

■ MYDAS FLIES

Characteristics Mydas flies have smooth bodies and are black in color. Their orange antennae may end in a club shape.

Life cycle, diet, and habitat Little is known of their life cycle, except that females lay their eggs in soil. The larvae eat beetle larvae. They are found in warm, sandy regions.

LIQUID SPONGER
House flies vomit saliva over their food to dissolve it, sopping up the mush with their sponge-like mouthparts.

MYDAS MIMICS
Some mydas flies mimic hoverflies or spider-hunting wasps. After mating, the female lays her eggs in soil.

IN THE FLESH
The streamlined shape of these blowfly maggots allows them to burrow quickly into decaying flesh.

■ HOVER FLIES

Characteristics So called because they can hover and dart among flowers, hover flies sport yellow stripes, spots, or bands. They are wasplike in shape, with large eyes and short antennae.

Life cycle, diet, and habitat Females lay eggs where their larvae will feed, in a variety of habitats, including boggy pools and heathland. Some larvae eat aphids or scale insects; others feed on plants and fungi. Adults eat nectar. Many species are important plant pollinators.

■ SOLDIER AND HORSE FLIES

Characteristics Soldier flies are slightly flattened, with metallic markings. Males have large eyes. Some species are aquatic. Horse flies are hairless, with patterned, sometimes iridescent eyes. The female's mouthparts can cut skin.

Life cycle, diet, and habitat Soldier flies lay their eggs on the surface of water or in dung, leaf litter, or soil. Adults live in a variety of habitats. Horse flies lay eggs in soil and rotten wood.

DARTING FLIGHT
Hover flies (right) are often seen darting and hovering over flowers. Their colors mimic those of wasps, giving them protection from predators.

SOLDIERING ON
Some aquatic soldier fly larvae can survive in salty water or in hot springs.

DARK HORSE
Certain horse fly species transmit damaging viruses to cattle and other livestock.

Caddis Flies

Number of species: 8,000

Length: 1/16–1 1/2 in (2–40 mm)

■ CHARACTERISTICS
Caddis flies are closely related
to moths and butterflies
(Order Lepidoptera), but are
distinguished by having short
hairs on their wings instead of
scales. They hold their wings
over their body like a roof
when at rest. During flight, the
hindwings and forewings are
connected by curved hairs.

SNAPSHOT

ORDER FEATURES **Mothlike
appearance; hairs on wings**
DIET **Larvae eat insect and plant
matter; adults may take liquids;
some are non-feeding**
LIFE CYCLE **Metamorphosis is
complete; eggs laid in water**
HABITAT **Adults found near
ponds, streams, marshes, and
bogs; larvae are aquatic**
DISTRIBUTION **Worldwide**

Most caddis flies are drably
colored; some have black, gray,
or white speckles. They have an
elongate body with triangular
wings, and a small head with
large, compound eyes. The long,
slender antennae consist of many
segments. Adults have chewing
mouthparts, but they are reduced,
and used only for drinking water
and nectar.

■ LIFE CYCLE AND DIET
Caddis flies undergo complete
metamorphosis. Eggs are
deposited in water, sometimes
in gelatinous masses, and
attached to water plants. The
larvae are active, sometimes
sucking the juices of water plants,
or eating debris, algae, and small
organisms. The aquatic larvae
pupate inside a case—often
characteristic of the species—
constructed from wood, leaves,
sand, or stone. The particles are
melded together with silk from
the salivary glands. Net-spinning
caddis fly larvae spin a cup-
shaped net between stones to
ensnare algae and small

AQUATIC COCOONS
Caddis fly larvae pupate underwater, inside their case, finally emerging and undertaking a final molt to adulthood.

organisms. The larval cases of northern caddis flies look like small log cabins. Adults are nocturnal and short-lived.

◼ HABITAT
Caddis flies are found near sunny ponds and streams, and in temporary pools and bogs.

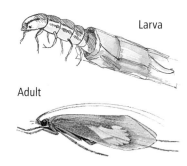

Larva

Adult

IN THE TUBE
Caddis fly larvae encase themselves in tubes made of sand, sticks, or leaves for protection. Adults are nocturnal and only live long enough to breed and lay eggs.

LEPIDOPTERA
127 families

Moths and Butterflies

Number of species: 180,000

Wingspan: 1/16–12½ in (2–320 mm)

■ CHARACTERISTICS
The name Lepidoptera, which
means "scaly wing," refers to
the millions of tiny, overlapping,
colored scales covering the
wings and body of all moths
and butterflies. The scales are
actually flat, hollow hairs. Many
are filled with pigment absorbed
from the insect's food; others
reflect light to produce a metallic
sheen. For all their variety in
color and pattern, the Lepidoptera
are remarkably uniform in their
morphology. Of the 180,000
species in this order, moths
outnumber butterflies ten to
one. Both moths and butterflies
have two pairs of wings that
beat in unison. When flying,
the forewings and hindwings link
together with tiny hooks. At rest,
butterflies hold their wings folded
up over their backs; moths rest

MOTH OR BUTTERFLY?
Moths and butterflies (below) can be
distinguished from each other by looking
at antennae: Butterflies have threadlike
antennae, ending in a club, whereas
most moths have feathery antennae.

88 butterfly

Ornate tiger
moth

TIGER MOTH
Some tiger moths (right) can detect
bat sonar with special sense organs,
and fly off to avoid capture.

with their wings spread flat. Moths mostly fly at night and have elaborately plumed or feathery antennae. Butterflies are daytime fliers and their slender, threadlike antennae are clubbed at the tips. Most butterflies have mouthparts that form a long tube, or proboscis, which can uncurl to feed on nectar and coil away again when not in use. Some moths have short, stabbing mouthparts; in some short-lived species they may be absent.

Lepidopterans have compound eyes that are sensitive to color patterns and to movement of

flowers; they are also sensitive to other moths and butterflies.

■ LIFE CYCLE AND DIET
Moths and butterflies undergo complete metamorphosis. Courtship may involve flying displays and pheromones. The scent signals are detected by the mate's antennae. After mating, the eggs are scattered on the ground or laid on plants. The larvae, called caterpillars, are mainly plant-eaters, with strong, chewing mouthparts, three pairs of legs on the thorax, and a number of abdominal prolegs; the prolegs have minute hooks to help to grip onto plants. Adults drink nectar, fruit juice, and tree sap. Caterpillars pupate in an underground, silk-lined chamber, encased in a silk cocoon, inside a seed or plant stem, or in a bare case called a chrysalis.

WITCHETTY GRUBS
The larvae of carpenter moths are called witchetty grubs. They live in the roots of certain trees and are eaten by Australian Aboriginals as a sought-after delicacy.

WELL SPOTTED
Hidden by the forewings when the owl moth is at rest, its eyespots are revealed when danger threatens (above).

CHEMICAL DEFENSE
Caterpillars (below) defend themselves from predators with toxins, "horns" that release a foul smell, or stinging, hairlike spines, like those of this silk moth larva.

■ HABITAT
Moths and butterflies are found on all continents, except Antarctica. In alpine areas, where temperatures are too cold for night-flying, moths have adapted to fly and feed during the day. They live in well-vegetated areas or wherever host plants grow.

HANGING AROUND
The bagworm caterpillar incorporates twigs and other debris into its cocoon design. It can then pupate unnoticed among the tree branches.

■ TIGER MOTHS
Characteristics These moths have thick, hairy bodies and bright red, yellow, orange, and black coloration.
Life cycle, diet, and habitat Females lay their eggs around the host plants. Many of the caterpillars are hairy and poisonous. They mainly feed at night on a wide variety of plants and live among foliage.

■ SILK MOTHS AND CLOTHES MOTHS
Characteristics Silk moths are pale cream or brown, with a profusion of hairs. They do not have functional mouthparts. Clothes moths are tiny, dull-brown scavengers that feed on a wide range of organic material, such as fabric, wool textiles, and skins. They are significant pests.

CRAWLING PROCESSION
Processionary moth caterpillars are the larvae of noctuid moths. They follow each other in single file.

COOL CAT
The vaporer
moth caterpillar
(a noctuid) is armed
with a battery of hairs
that can irritate skin.

Life cycle, diet, and habitat
Silk moths lay their eggs on food
plants suitable for their larvae.
The caterpillars pupate within
a silk cocoon, and these are used
in commercial silk production.
They live in well-vegetated areas.
Clothes moths live among cloth.

■ CARPENTER MOTHS
Characteristics These moths are
cream or brown, with a large body
and speckled or spotted wings.
Life cycle, diet, and habitat
The eggs are laid on bark. The
caterpillars tunnel into wood and
eat the fibers. They pupate inside
cocoons made of silk and chewed
wood fibers. They are found in
wooded areas.

■ NOCTUID MOTHS
Characteristics The largest
family in the order, these
nocturnal moths have quite
narrow forewings and broader
hindwings. Noctuids usually have
dull forewings and often more
brightly colored hindwings.
Life cycle, diet, and habitat Eggs
are laid singly or in numbers in
the soil or on host plants. The
caterpillars attack plants, chewing
their way inside. Many are
serious pests of crops, such as
maize, cotton, and rice. Adults of
some species have unusual food
preferences; the vampire moth
pierces the skin of mammals and
feeds on their blood. Noctuids
live in a variety of habitats.

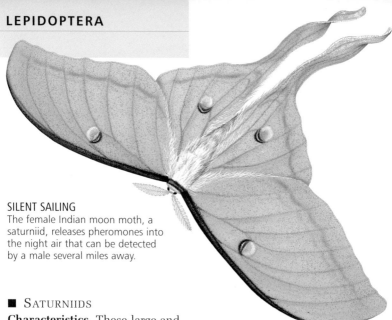

SILENT SAILING
The female Indian moon moth, a saturniid, releases pheromones into the night air that can be detected by a male several miles away.

■ SATURNIIDS

Characteristics These large and impressive moths display a variety of colors and patterns, including prominent eyespots and wing patches. Pale green saturniids with long tails and eyespots are known as moon or luna moths. Other well-known species include the royal and emperor moths. The world's largest moth, *Attacus atlas*, is a saturniid. Many species in the genus *Attacus* are protected in some countries. Males have expansive, feathery antennae to help them detect the scent signals of the females; the females' antennae are threadlike. All these moths are night-fliers.

Life cycle, diet, and habitat Females lay their eggs on foliage. The larvae feed on a wide variety of trees and shrubs. Cocoons may be attached to twigs or left among leaves on the ground. Adult saturniids are non-feeding and they do not possess working mouthparts. They live in wooded areas and are often seen fluttering around street lights.

POWERFUL JAWS
The hickory horned devil is the caterpillar of the regal moth, a saturniid. The powerful muscles of its large mandibles can chew through the leaves of hickory and walnut trees.

LEPIDOPTERA

■ HAWK MOTHS

Characteristics Hawk moths are renowned for their powerful and speedy flight. They can hover at flowers to suck nectar with their long proboscis. The proboscis is curled up under the body when they are not feeding. They have a thick, rounded body that tapers to a point.

Life cycle, diet, and habitat The eggs are laid singly on plants. The caterpillars eat the foliage of host plants. Most larvae have a soft spine at the end of the body, resulting in the common name of hornworms. Some are pests of tomatoes and other crops. They usually pupate in the ground. Adults are nectar-feeders; the

BAD TASTE
The red spots on this five-spotted burnet moth advertise that it has an unpleasant taste, and predators tend to avoid it.

death's head hawk moth eats honey from hives. Most adults feed at dusk or at night; some feed during the day. They inhabit subtropical and tropical environments, wherever their host plants are found.

■ BURNET MOTHS

Characteristics Also known as foresters, these dark-bodied moths often have bright or metallic blue, green or red

HAWK MOTHS
During the time from hatching to pupation, this sphinx moth caterpillar (left), like other caterpillars, increases its size about 30,000 times. Hawk moths (right) are often so heavy that they cannot land on flowers. Instead, they hover like bumblebees to collect nectar.

coloration. They have thick antennae and small, hairy bumps above the eyes. Many species display warning coloration to signal that they contain poisons and that they are harmful to eat.

Life cycle, diet, and habitat Females lay their eggs on suitable food plants for their hatched larvae. The larvae pupate inside an elongate cocoon. These moths feed and fly during the day.

■ SKIPPERS

Characteristics Skippers are daytime feeders and fliers. They are considered to be butterflies and take their common name from their distinctive, strong and darting flight. They have a thick body and a long or curved club

IN THE WOODS
The golden-banded skipper prefers moist, wooded areas near wetlands.

on the tip of their antennae.
The forewings are triangular;
a few species have long tails
on their hindwings, similar to
those of luna moths.

Life cycle, diet, and habitat
Skippers lay single eggs on host
plants. The larvae feed at night
on leaves, herbs, and grasses, and
usually live in a shelter made
from rolled-up leaves. Adults
feed on nectar. Because they feed

ON THE WING
At rest, many skippers, such as this
least skipper, hold their forewings and
hindwings at slightly different angles.

at flowers, they cross-pollinate
many plants. Some species fly
great distances. Skippers live
in a variety of habitats, usually
near grassland and farmland.
They are found worldwide,
except in New Zealand.

■ HAIRSTREAKS, BLUES AND COPPERS

Characteristics These butterflies have a small, slender body and show a wide variety of wing colors and patterns. The upper side of the wings may be brown or orange, or iridescent blue, copper, or purple; the undersides are dull. Males and females are often differently colored. Some blues and coppers have white, hairlike scales on the body and fringing on their wings.

Hairstreaks usually have streamers on their hindwings that may be long and trailing, or short and dark-edged. Many hairstreak species are commonly seen perched on plants, rubbing their hindwings back and forth.

Life cycle, diet, and habitat Females lay their eggs on host plants. The caterpillars may feed on plants or on small insects, such as aphids. The caterpillars of many species have "honey glands" on their abdomen. These glands secrete a sweet liquid (honeydew) that attracts ants. A beneficial relationship results for both insects: The caterpillar gains protection from parasitic wasp attack and the ant derives a regular source of nutrition. Larvae pupate on plants or underground. They live around host plants or in ants' nests, in warmer regions. Some species of coppers are found in vacant lots, landfill, fields, and gardens.

NECTAR FEAST
The roemer acacia, found in North America's southwest, provides nectar for butterflies, such as the marine blue.

LUSTROUS COPPER
This lustrous copper (above) shows the hairlike fringing of the wings displayed by a number of species.

BUCKWHEAT MEAL
Bramble green hair-streak caterpillars (left) feed on the leaves of wild buckwheat. They are found on the west coast of North America.

■ BRUSH-FOOTS

Characteristics These butterflies, also known as nymphalids, vary greatly in color and size. The front legs are markedly reduced, hence their common name. The upper side of the wings is brightly colored and patterned; the underside has camouflage coloration. Members of this family include the following well-known species: red admiral, viceroy, monarch, painted lady, mourning cloak (Camberwell beauty), blue morpho, and

WIDE-RANGERS
Fritillaries (Nymphalidae) inhabit a wide range of habitats, including alpine meadows, roadsides, and marshy areas.

fritillaries. Some fritillaries are sluggish fliers; others have strong flying abilities, and sometimes travel long distances. Monarchs and painted ladies are famous for their migratory habits. The monarch migrates thousands of miles, from Canada to Mexico.

Life cycle, diet, and habitat
Females lay their ribbed eggs on trees, shrubs, and herbaceous plants. In temperate regions,

BLUE BEAUTY
The iridescent colors on the wings of the exquisite blue morpho are produced not by pigmentation, but by bending light.

some adult species hibernate during the harsh winter months. Brush-foots live in a variety of habitats—usually forests or meadows with abundant foliage—from the arctic tundra to tropical rainforests.

■ SWALLOWTAILS

Characteristics Swallowtails include the largest and most strikingly colored butterflies. They typically have dark wings, with spots and patches of green, blue, yellow, or orange. Many species have tails on their hindwings. Most swallowtails are fast and powerful fliers. The larvae have a forked scent organ, called an osmeterium, on their head, which secretes a foul-smelling substance. The caterpillars of some species, such as the giant swallowtail *Papilio cresphontes,* eat citrus leaves, and their osmeterium exudes an orange scent. The most spectacular members of this family (Papilionidae) are the birdwing butterflies from the tropical regions of Southeast Asia. Some are so large (wingspans of 8 inches [20 cm]) that early butterfly collectors would shoot them with fine shot. Birdwings are now protected by law.

Life-cycle, diet, and habitat The round eggs are laid on a variety of host plants. Caterpillars pupate on host plants. Most swallowtails live in tropical regions, in open or shaded flower-filled areas.

MIMICRY
The black swallowtail (left) mimics the color and flight patterns of the pipe vine swallowtail, a butterfly that predators avoid.

TRUE BEAUTY
At nearly 6 inches (15 cm) wide, the giant swallowtail (right) is one of the largest butterflies in North America.

■ SULFURS AND WHITES
Characteristics These common
butterflies have representatives
in most parts of the world. They
usually have white, yellow, or
orange wings. The wing scales
are filled with pigments that are
a by-product of the caterpillar's
food. The caterpillars are usually
hairless and green, with a yellow
line down each side. Some adults
migrate in large numbers.

ORANGE AND WHITE
Orange sulfurs (above) can often be
seen drinking from puddles. The cabbage
white butterfly (below) is unpopular with
gardeners and farmers; its larvae can
strip cabbage plants bare.

Life cycle, diet, and habitat
Many species engage in spiral
flights that may be associated
with mating. Females usually
lay elongate eggs on host plants.
One of the most common species
in this family (Pieridae) is the
cabbage white. Cabbage white
caterpillars feed on cabbage
leaves and are serious agricultural
pests. Whites and sulfurs are very

FLOWER FAVORITES
The clouded sulfur is a strong flier.
It favors feeding from the flowers
of the alfalfa and other legumes.

common and are often found
sipping fluids from around
puddles and bird droppings.
The caterpillars feed mostly on
legumes and clovers. They are
found in a wide range of habitats.

Bees, Wasps, Ants, and Sawflies

Number of species: 198,000

Length: 1/128–2 3/4 in (0.25–70 mm)

SPRING POLLINATOR
The hairy-legged mining bee is a vital pollinator of many spring flowers. Pollen is trapped on its body hairs as it feeds.

■ CHARACTERISTICS
Hymenopterans are vital plant pollinators, predators, and parasites in the world's eco-systems. Many species in this large order are also social insects. All adults have chewing mouthparts, which for some species act as tools for digging, building nests, and slicing up food. Most have two pairs of membranous wings that join together with small hooks during flight, and large compound eyes. With the exception of sawflies, the thorax and abdomen are divided by a constricted "waist," called a pedicel. The ovipositor of female bees, ants, and social wasps has evolved into a stinger with associated poison glands. Hymenopterans range in size from the fairyfly wasp, so small it could fly through the eye of a needle, to the spider-eating wasp, measuring 2 3/4 inches (70 mm).

SNAPSHOT		
ORDER FEATURES	**Usually constricted "waist" between thorax and abdomen, forewings and hindwings joined by hooks; chewing mouthparts; many groups are social**	
DIET	**Insect and plant matter**	
LIFE CYCLE	**Metamorphosis is complete; eggs laid in nests**	
HABITAT	**All terrestrial habitats**	
DISTRIBUTION	**Worldwide**	

■ LIFE CYCLE AND DIET
All hymenopterans undergo complete metamorphosis. Fertilized eggs produce females

NO SWEAT
Also called sweat bees, members of the family Halictidae brood their eggs underground, within cells that are waterproofed with a special bee secretion.

LEAF-CUTTERS
Female leaf-cutter bees clip out circular pieces of leaf with their jaws. These are taken back to their nests where they are fashioned into tube-shaped cells for the eggs and larvae.

QUEEN BEE
Workers raise a new queen inside a special, pendulous queen cell. She is fed a bee secretion called royal jelly.

each hindleg called a corbiculum. Many species have black and yellow banding, or a metallic blue or green sheen. Honeybees are highly social and live in colonies of up to 60,000 individuals. In contrast, bumblebees form small colonies, usually on or under the ground. A typical honeybee hive includes the egg-laying queen, workers (sterile females), who tend the young and the queen, find food, and look after the hive, and drones (males).

Life cycle, diet, and habitat
Honeybees have special glands on the underside of their bodies that ooze a waxy substance. They scrape this off and use it to make honeycomb—double-sided wax combs divided into hexagonal cells. These cells are used to brood the bee larvae and store honey and pollen. A queen can lay over 1,000 eggs a day,

and unfertilized eggs result in males. Adults are usually fruit- or nectar-eaters; larvae eat insect or plant matter.

■ HABITAT
Hymenopterans live on all continents except Antarctica. Many groups are adapted to arid and semi-arid regions.

■ HONEYBEES AND ALLIES
Characteristics Honeybees and bumblebees are the best-known species in this family (Apidae). Most females have a pollen-storing basket on the outside of

POLLEN BASKETS
Worker honeybees collect pollen in basket-like notches on their back legs. Pollen is taken back to the hive and stored for periods when food is scarce.

every day of her life. She lays two kinds of egg: fertilized eggs develop into workers or queens, and unfertilized eggs become drones. Eggs hatch in approximately three days and the larvae are fed by workers for six days before being capped inside cells for a pupation lasting twelve to fourteen days. Future queens are fed an enriched diet consisting mainly of royal jelly, a creamy substance formed by special glands in the heads of the young worker bees. When the hive has reached its size limits, a young queen flies off to found a new colony, followed by a swarm of as many as 70,000 workers.

Unlike wasps, honeybees and their allies are strictly vegetarian, feeding only on nectar and pollen. Workers use a special dance to communicate the direction, distance, and abundance of a food supply.

Honeybees and their allies are found worldwide, except in sub-Saharan Africa. They live and feed in flower-rich habitats.

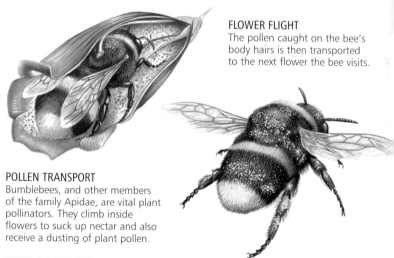

FLOWER FLIGHT
The pollen caught on the bee's body hairs is then transported to the next flower the bee visits.

POLLEN TRANSPORT
Bumblebees, and other members of the family Apidae, are vital plant pollinators. They climb inside flowers to suck up nectar and also receive a dusting of plant pollen.

■ MINING BEES
Characteristics Most members of this family are solitary. Many species have a hairy thorax and abdomen, and are red-brown or dark brown to black in color.
Life cycle, diet, and habitat Females make cells in soil burrows, each supplied with pollen and honey, into which they lay their eggs. They live worldwide, except Australia.

OVERFED
Parasitic bees, such as cuckoo bees, lay eggs in the larval cells of other bees. The cuckoo bee's larvae eat the host's larvae, as well as their stored food supply.

■ CUCKOO AND DIGGER BEES
Characteristics Most cuckoo bees are solitary and wasplike in appearance, with black and yellow coloration. The solitary digger bees are round and hairy.

Life cycle, diet, and habitat
Cuckoo bees parasitize the larvae of soil-nesting bees. Digger bees build nests in the ground, providing their larval cells with honey and pollen. Both these bees are found near flowers.

■ HALICTID BEES

Characteristics Also called sweat bees, most species are dark brown or black, but some species have metallic green or blue coloration. Usually solitary, some show a degree of societal structure.

Life cycle, diet, and habitat
Females lay their eggs in underground tunnels or in rotten wood. The larvae that mature are all females and they make tunnels as offshoots of their mother's

VELVET ANT
The females of this wasp family (Mutillidae) are wingless, covered in velvety hairs, and ant-like in appearance.

JEWEL THIEF
This brilliantly colored jewel wasp is also called a cuckoo wasp. Its larvae steal the food provided for the host's larvae.

tunnel, raising a brood without mating. These larvae develop into males, and then mate with a brood laid by the original female. Halictid bees are found worldwide in flower-rich habitats.

■ VELVET ANTS

Characteristics These "ants" are actually wasps that take their common name from the appearance of the female, who is covered with soft, velvety hairs and is wingless. Males have fully developed wings.

Life cycle, diet, and habitat
Velvet ants parasitize the nests of other wasps and bees. A female seeks out the nest of a suitable host, bites open a larval cell, lays her own egg inside, and reseals it.

■ JEWEL WASPS

Characteristics These wasps are bright metallic green, red, or blue in color. Their body surface is

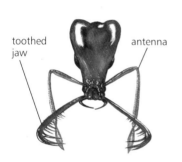

INSECT ILLUSIONS

Ant colonies are controlled largely by chemical signals. This ant-nest beetle (right) secretes a chemical to fool ants into accepting it as a colony member, and then eats their eggs and larvae.

toothed jaw   antenna

HEAD AND TAIL

The trap-jaw ants, a tropical genus, have large and menacing jaws, and they also are capable of inflicting a painful sting.

hard and dimpled, which protects them from wasp and bee stings. They are also called ruby wasps, because of their coloration, or cuckoo wasps, because they steal the food that the host species has provided for its larvae.

Life cycle, diet, and habitat
Jewel wasps parasitize solitary bee or wasp larvae. The females lay an egg in the host's nest, and the larva eats the host's larvae and food provisions.

■ ANTS

Characteristics Ants are members of a highly social family of insects (Formicidae). Some ant colonies contain only a few hundred individuals; others, such as driver ants, have colonies consisting of more than 20 million insects. Most species are brown, red-brown, or black in color, although there are yellow and green species. The second abdominal segment is constricted to form the characteristic "waist,"

HEADSTRONG BULLDOG
The mandibles of the bulldog ant are large and heavily toothed. After ambushing its katydid prey, the ant may sting its victim with the poisonous stinger on its abdomen.

or pedicel possessed by most members of this order. The pedicel has a spiny process or a small, scale-like bump. Ants have large heads and large eyes, and generally three ocelli. The antennae have 11 or 12 segments, and may be long in some species. Most have chewing mouthparts.

Like social bees, ants have very sophisticated sensory systems. Pheromones are used to recognize individual colony members and the queen is able to control the reproductive status of her workers using these pheromone signals.

Members of individual castes have different physical attributes: The queen is large with a rounded abdomen; reproductive males and females have wings at certain stages of their lives; workers are small and compact; and soldiers often have large heads or enlarged mandibles.

Ants protect themselves from attack by stinging and biting, or by spraying formic acid from a gland at the rear of their abdomen. When the nest is attacked, workers carry the larvae to safety deeper underground.

Life cycle, diet, and habitat Each year a new colony is founded by a winged female and male. When conditions are optimal, these flying ants swarm out of the nest in search of new homes. The male dies soon after mating, but the female lives for many years. She never leaves the nest, and continues to produce huge numbers of eggs. Most of the queen's eggs hatch as sterile female worker ants. These workers collect food, look after the nest, raise the young, and tend the queen.

Most ants build permanent nests, and spend their lives in the same area. Nests are usually

BIG-HEADED ANTS
Ant societies are divided into castes, each with a defined purpose within the colony. Winged males fertilize the queen's eggs, workers tend the young, and soldiers protect the nest from harm.

Queen

Worker

Male

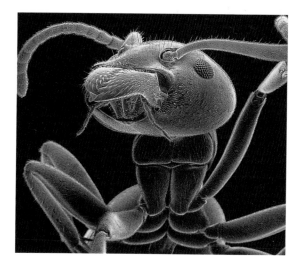

IN THE DARK
This worker ant lives in the darkness of the nest. It has small compound eyes, containing only a few hundred eyelets, and relies on other sensory signals, including pheromones, to communicate with fellow workers.

constructed from soil, leaves, or wood. Army ants and driver ants, however, form marauding hordes, sweeping across the ground, killing and eating any other insects in their path.

Not all ants are carnivores. Adult bulldog ants also eat tree sap and honeydew, and leaf-cutter ants grow fungus gardens (see page 98). Honey ants feed nectar to specialized workers; the workers store the nectar in their balloon-like abdomens.

Ants play an important role in ecosystems. Some species help to break down plant material and refine soil; others spread seed or help to decompose carrion. In contrast, some species—fire ants and leaf-cutter ants, for example— are serious crop pests.

Ants live in all habitats, including desert and alpine areas.

Soldier

■ SOCIAL WASPS

Characteristics Probably the best-known members of this large family (Vespidae) are the hornets, yellow jackets, and paper wasps. They can be recognized by the way they hold their wings when at rest—they are rolled along the length of the wing and held out slightly to each side of the body. (Other wasps hold their wings flat over their back.) Many species are social, making a papery nest for their colony from chewed up

DIRTY WORK
Mud daubers are solitary wasps. They construct small nests using pellets of mud, molded into place by the wasp's mandibles.

wood fibers (see page 67). Mason wasps make under-ground, mud-lined nests.

Life cycle, diet, and habitat Adult wasps feed on nectar and rotting fruit; the larvae, called grubs, eat spiders and insects. Yellow jacket and paper wasp colonies have queens to lay eggs and workers to rear young, as well as overlapping generations.

■ DIGGER WASPS

Characteristics Also known as mud daubers and sand wasps, these solitary wasps nest in plants, soil, or rotting wood; some nest inside the burrows of insects. Most have yellow markings or a metallic blue-green sheen.

A HORNET'S NEST
Hornets nest inside hollow trees, with only a few hundred individuals in the colony. True to the adage, they get aggressive if their nest is threatened.

FRUIT DRINK
Worker social wasps hunt for insects to feed their colony's larvae, but they will also take fruit juice for themselves.

PARALYZING POWER
A spider-hunting wasp avoids a tarantula's fangs by stabbing it with a long stinger that administers a paralyzing poison.

Life cycle, diet, and habitat
Females capture an insect or
spider, paralyze it with a sting,
and take it to a nest. The prey is
buried, along with a single egg.
The emerging wasp larva feeds
on the stored prey. Adult digger
wasps eat a variety of insect prey,
including butterflies. They are
found in a range of habitats.

■ SPIDER-HUNTING WASPS
Characteristics Some members of
this family (Pompilidae) are very
large. Many are dark blue or black
in color, with wing patterns
ranging from white patches to
a purplish sheen. They have a
slender body and long legs.

HEARING MOVEMENT
A torymid wasp uses its antennae to feel
the vibrations of insect larvae as they
move within their nesting chamber. The
wasp uses its long ovipositor to reach
inside, laying an egg on the host larvae.

Life cycle, diet, and habitat The
females of some species search
for spider prey on the wing. They
use their strong poison to subdue
the spider, and then place it
inside a mud nest. They lay a
single egg, usually on the spider's
abdomen, and the larvae hatch
and eat their host. These wasps
live in tropical areas, in habitats
where spiders are found.

■ ICHNEUMON WASPS
Characteristics The distinctive
feature of most of these slender
wasps is the long, thin ovipositor
used for drilling into tree trunks
or tree galls. Most have long,
slender antennae. They are
brown to black in color, with
either brown and black or yellow
and black patterns.
Life cycle, diet, and habitat
Using their ovipositor,
ichneumon wasps lay their
eggs in or on the larvae of other
insects, usually beetles, moths,
and sawflies. They live in the
world's warmer regions, in a
wide range of habitats wherever
their hosts occur.

■ TORYMID WASPS

Characteristics Many torymid wasps have shiny, metallic green or blue coloration, and a long, slender ovipositor.

Life cycle, diet, and habitat The ovipositor is used to parasitize gall-forming flies and wasps. Plant-eating species lay their eggs

FINE DRILLING
An ichneumon wasp's ovipositor is as fine as a human hair. It is, however, strong enough to drill through wood.

in the seeds of certain trees, where their larvae develop. They are found in a variety of habitats, wherever hosts can be found.

■ SAWFLIES

Characteristics Sawflies are considered the most primitive member of this order. They do not have the marked narrowing and fusing of abdominal segments displayed in other families of hymenopterans. The ovipositor of female sawflies is, as their common name suggests, saw-like.

SPOTTED SURPRISE
Figwort sawflies resemble spotted caterpillars. This warning coloration gives them some protection from predators.

Life cycle, diet, and habitat
Females cut slits in the leaves and shoots of plants and lay their eggs inside. The larvae feed on the outside of the plant, and pupate inside a silk cocoon. Horntails use their ovipositor to drill into trees, laying eggs and, at the same time, infecting the tree with a fungus. The larvae eat both the wood and fungus before pupating inside a cocoon composed of silk and chewed wood fibers. Some larvae produce substances to repel predators.

OVER-EATING
Adult pergid sawflies lay their eggs on Australian eucalypt trees. The larvae are voracious eaters, and can cause the total defoliation of a forest.

ON GUARD
These pergid sawfly larvae cock up their tails in a defensive posture, and regurgitate their stomach contents to deter predators.

KINDS OF ARACHNIDS

*An informative, illustrated guide
to the major orders of spiders,
scorpions, mites, and their allies*

Spiders

FOR MOST PEOPLE, spiders arouse mixed emotions. Many of us marvel at their intricate and glistening webs, but may also be terrified by their painful or potentially fatal bites. The most familiar of all arachnids, spiders play an essential role in Earth's ecosystems by keeping insect populations balanced. Spiders display a broad range of adaptations and behaviors, and have a vast, worldwide distribution. These colorful and resourceful creatures certainly deserve closer inspection.

Spiders

Number of species: 40,000

Length: $1/32$–$3 1/2$ in (1–90 mm)

HIDING PLACE
This long-jawed orb weaver lies along grass stems, head pointing downward, to hide from predators.

SNAPSHOT	
ORDER FEATURES	Relatively short pedipalps; first pair of legs similar in size to others; non-segmented abdomen; silk organs
DIET	Mostly insects; occasionally small vertebrates
LIFE CYCLE	Round eggs laid in silk cocoon; some carry young
HABITAT	All habitats (except marine), including houses
DISTRIBUTION	Worldwide

■ CHARACTERISTICS

Like insects, spiders are one of the most abundant groups in the animal kingdom. They are characterized by their general body shape and by their ability to spin silk into webs and other structures. They range in size from money spiders no bigger than a pinprick, to tarantulas nearly twice the size of a human hand. All spiders have hinged, hollow fangs at the end of their jaws, called chelicerae, through which they can inject poison into prey. Fangs not only bite, but they also hold and crush prey. The cephalothorax and abdomen are joined together by a stalk, called the pedicel. Spiders have a variable number of eyes (six to

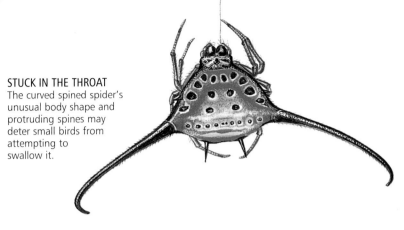

STUCK IN THE THROAT
The curved spined spider's unusual body shape and protruding spines may deter small birds from attempting to swallow it.

eight) on the cephalothorax. A spider's pedipalps are important sensory organs; in males, they also transfer sperm to females. Each of the eight walking legs is made up of seven segments.

Spiders have an unsegmented abdomen, which carries the silk-spinning organs called spinnerets. Spiders build an enormous variety of webs in which they catch flying insect prey. Webs vary from tripwires and untidy cobwebs to intricate orbs. A high percentage of spiders do not weave webs, but instead rely on stealth and speed to hunt their prey. Some chase down their preferred prey; others use a "sit-and-wait" strategy, pouncing when prey is in range.

■ LIFE CYCLE AND DIET
Some spiders have elaborate courtship behaviors (see page 58). Most spiders lay their eggs in a silk sac (up to 1,000 eggs in some tarantula species). Many carry these sacs with them until the eggs hatch; others camouflage them with debris and keep them in the web or buried in leaf litter. The hatched young are called spiderlings. They do not undergo metamorphosis, but molt at periods during their lifetime to increase in size and to reach sexual maturity. Many leave the silk egg sacs via silken threads that float them to the ground.

Most spiders eat small insect prey; larger species tackle fish, frogs, birds, and small mammals.

Spiders cannot chew, but instead inject digestive enzymes and paralyzing poison into their prey, dissolving their body tissues and sucking up the resultant liquid. Prey items that are not eaten immediately may be wrapped in a silk shroud and stored for later consumption.

BODY SPOTS
This male eresid spider has a distinctive, orange abdomen with black spots. They are found in Africa, Europe, and Asia.

■ HABITAT

Spiders live on all continents except Antarctica, in forests, grasslands, deserts, cliffs, caves, fresh water, and in houses. Most are nocturnal, although some are active during the day. They live among moss and low vegetation, such as grasses and flowers, in bushes, and in the lower foliage of trees. Many web-builders make silk-lined burrows to rest in during the day; nocturnal hunters shelter under stones or debris.

■ ORB-WEB SPIDERS
AND FUNNEL WEAVERS

Characteristics Orb-web spiders have a large abdomen that is often distinctively patterned or strangely shaped. They have eight eyes. Females are often larger than males. They make a web with a central hub, criss-

UNDERWATER DINING
The water spider actively hunts for insects and then brings them back into its silk-shrouded bubble to be eaten.

crossed with radiating lines and spirals. Funnel weavers have long legs and many hairs on their bodies. Their cephalothorax bears eight eyes. They construct a funnel-shaped shelter on the edge of a flat web.

Life cycle, diet, and habitat
Orb-web spiders have complex courtships. They attach their silk egg sacs to bark, inside the web, or conceal them in leaf litter. Funnel weavers keep their egg sac in the web. The newly hatched young may be fed regurgitated food. Both spiders live in forests, grasslands, and gardens.

■ WATER SPIDER
Characteristics This spider—the only species in its family—lives mostly underwater. Its third and fourth pairs of legs have specialized tufts of long hairs that help it trap air. The water spider makes a domed diving bell out of silk and fills it with bubbles of air from the surface. It stays within the dome during the day, leaving only to find food at night.

Life cycle, diet, and habitat Eggs are laid and then wrapped in silk and placed in the top of the bell. Water spiders capture small fish and tadpoles and eat them inside the bell. This spider lives in still or slow-flowing water, in parts of Asia and in Europe.

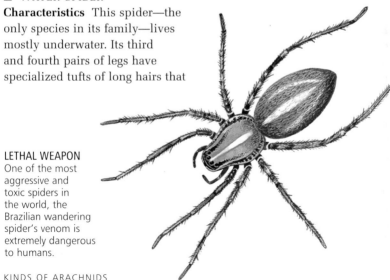

LETHAL WEAPON
One of the most aggressive and toxic spiders in the world, the Brazilian wandering spider's venom is extremely dangerous to humans.

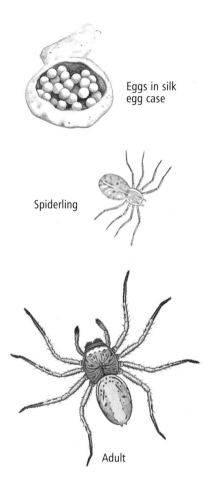

■ ERESID SPIDERS
Characteristics These round, hairy spiders have a squarish cephalothorax with eight eyes. The males of some species are brightly colored. Some species build webs in the ground, attached to funnel-shaped webs on the surface.
Life cycle, diet, and habitat
Females carry their egg sacs on their body or keep them inside their burrow. Eresids live among shrubs and on the ground in parts of Asia, Europe, and Africa.

■ HUNTSMAN SPIDERS
Characteristics Most species have mottled coloration. They have long legs relative to their body, which are covered in stout spines. They have eight eyes.
Life cycle, diet, and habitat
These spiders have complex courtship rituals. The females hide egg sacs under bark or stones until the eggs hatch. They hunt at night, hiding under bark, stones, and vegetation during the day. They live mainly in warmer regions in various habitats.

Eggs in silk egg case

Spiderling

Adult

WATCHFUL MOTHER
Female huntsman spiders guard their egg sacs until the young are ready to hatch, months after laying them. She then opens the sac to release her spiderlings.

SPIDER

■ WANDERING SPIDERS

Characteristics Very similar in appearance to wolf spiders, these spiders are usually gray or brown, with a distinctive groove running lengthways on the cephalothorax. The toxin of some species is dangerous to humans.

Life cycle, diet, and habitat
Eggs are laid inside a silk case, carried under the female's body. Wandering spiders are active nocturnal hunters. They search for their prey on the ground and are usually found on low-growing shrubs, or on the ground.

■ WOLF SPIDERS

Characteristics These pale gray to dark brown spiders may have bands, or black spots, and thick, stout legs. They have eight eyes: four large and four small.

Life cycle, diet, and habitat
Wolf spiders may have complex courtship behavior, involving leg-lifting and other visual signals. Females of most species carry their egg sacs with them. When the eggs hatch, the mother carries the spiderlings on her body for a time, sometimes brushing them from her eyes so that she can see. These active hunters have excellent eyesight, searching for prey at night among leaf litter.

■ NURSERY-WEB SPIDERS

Characteristics Similar in some features to wolf spiders, nursery-web spiders are large and long-legged, with eight eyes. They

LEGS IN THE AIR
Male wolf spiders perform a courtship dance to impress a potential mate. If the dance is carried out satisfactorily, the female allows the male's advance.

vary in color from gray to dark brown, with brown or white legs covered with black hairs. The abdomen and cephalothorax have stripes running down each side.
Life cycle, diet, and habitat A female carries her silken egg sac in her chelicerae. Just before the eggs hatch, she spins a silk "tent" web to enclose the emerging spiderlings. She will guard them for a time, even chasing away small predators if they threaten. Adults run across the ground to catch prey. They live in a variety

EGGS ON THE MOVE
Female wolf spiders carry their egg sacs on their body, attached to their spinnerets, for extra protection.

of habitats, on the ground and at the water's edge. Some species are semi-aquatic, catching tadpoles, small fish, and insects at the surface.

■ JUMPING SPIDERS
Characteristics Jumping spiders are relatively small and mostly drably colored. Some have a

pattern of dark and light banding on their legs. They have eight eyes, four of which form a row on the cephalothorax. The two middle eyes are much larger than the rest. Their common name comes from their habit of jumping at prey. With their good vision, these daytime hunters stalk their prey at close range and then pounce on them.

Life cycle, diet, and habitat Most lay their eggs under stones and bark, and in vegetation, encased in a silk cell. Mothers guard the eggs until they hatch. They live in many habitats, including sunny spots on walls or on the ground.

SPLENDID VISION
Jumping spiders have relatively good vision. They can detect prey up to 8 inches (20 cm) away.

ONE GIANT LEAP
A jumping spider can leap four times the length of its own body. It often secures itself with a silk safety line.

■ CRAB SPIDERS
Characteristics These spiders get their common name from their crab-like appearance and the sideways movements of some species. Many have a broad abdomen. The first two pairs of legs, used to catch and grasp prey, are larger and armed with more spines than the other two pairs. Many crab spiders are colorful, often matching the pink, white, or yellow flowers that they hunt on. One common species spends its time among yellow or white flowers, and can alternate its color from one to the other so that it blends in with its surroundings.

Life cycle, diet, and habitat Crab spiders attach their egg sacs to plants and then guard them until they hatch. They feed on insects, especially those that visit flowers. Crab spiders are found mainly in gardens and meadows, around flowers, but also on vegetation.

SAFETY NET
A female nursery-web spider carries her egg sac until her young are ready to hatch. She then spins a nursery area out of silk to enclose and protect her spiderlings.

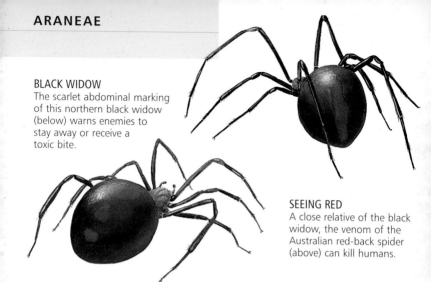

BLACK WIDOW
The scarlet abdominal marking of this northern black widow (below) warns enemies to stay away or receive a toxic bite.

SEEING RED
A close relative of the black widow, the venom of the Australian red-back spider (above) can kill humans.

■ COMB-FOOTED SPIDERS
Characteristics This family (Theridiidae) includes the infamous American black widow and the Australian red-back. They have a globular abdomen and are brown or black in color. Most are nocturnal hunters, moving along the ground in search of suitable prey. They build webs in vegetation, in cracks and crevices, and under buildings.
Life cycle, diet, and habitat After mating, females may eat the male, earning the black widow her name. They attach their egg sacs, containing up to 250 eggs, to their

webs. These spiders are found among vegetation, under stones and leaf litter, and in and around buildings.

■ TARANTULAS
Characteristics Members of this family (Theraphosidae) are large, hairy, nocturnal hunters, with pink, brown, white, red, or black markings. They have relatively poor vision, provided by a group

GRAB AND STAB
Camouflaged crab spiders lurk among flowers with their front legs wide open. They strike when prey comes into range.

of eight small eyes on the front of the cephalothorax. Some species, such as the Mexican red-legged tarantula, are ground-dwellers that actively hunt prey, usually after dusk. Using their large, downward-stabbing fangs, they

OPEN WIDE
Trapdoor spiders live in silk-lined burrows, with a silk door. They pounce on prey and eat it inside the burrow.

crush their victims and then suck up their body fluids. Tree-living species hunt among the foliage of forest trees. A tarantula's body hairs have microscopic barbed spines that make skin itch and burn. When threatened, it scrapes hairs off its abdomen and showers them on its enemy.

Life cycle, diet, and habitat
Females lay up to 1,000 eggs in a burrow. Most tarantulas hunt

on the ground, capturing arthropods, small frogs, and mice; tree-dwelling species eat insects and small reptiles. Tarantulas live in a variety of habitats, including deserts and forests.

OLD AGE
Most spiders have a life span of only 2 or 3 years, but some tropical tarantulas live to 17 years or more.

■ FUNNEL-WEB AND
   TRAPDOOR SPIDERS
Characteristics These usually dark brown spiders have six or eight eyes, and long spinnerets. They have large fangs and highly toxic venom, that may be fatal if antivenin is not administered quickly. Their silk-lined burrows incorporate a series of silken trip wires at the front, alerting them to nearby prey. Trapdoor spiders wait in their tunnels, just beneath their circular trapdoor made from silk and soil, ready to pounce on passing prey.
Life cycle, diet, and habitat Females lay disk-shaped eggs with a tough casing. They keep the eggs in their burrows until they hatch. They live in various habitats, in Asia, Australia, Africa, and North America.

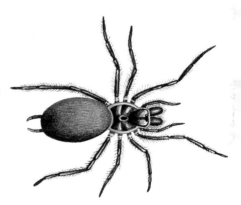

DANGEROUS MALE
The male Sydney funnel-web spider has extremely toxic venom. Its bite is far more deadly than that of the female.

Scorpions, Mites, and Allies

THIS DIVERSE COLLECTION OF ARACHNIDS includes the large and sometimes dangerous scorpions, the seldom-seen pseudoscorpions, and the tiny, parasitic mites and ticks. Many are considered serious pests of crops and livestock, and some carry debilitating diseases. Despite the enormous numbers of some—particularly the mites—little is known of their life histories.

Scorpions

Number of species: 1,400

Length: 5/16–8 1/4 in (80–210 mm)

(e). my ① favret

■ CHARACTERISTICS
Scorpions are the most ancient
group of arachnid. Like
spiders, scorpions have eight
walking legs attached to their
cephalothorax. They differ from
spiders in having an abdomen

divided into 12 segments. The
last five segments of the abdomen
make up the distinctive, mobile
"tail" or telson. The telson bears
a stinger and poison gland, which
is used to paralyze prey, and in
defense. The sting of some species
is lethal to humans. The modified
pedipalps, resembling large,
lobster-like pincers, are used to
seize and subdue prey. Scorpions
have 12 eyes; the main pair is
situated on top of the head and a

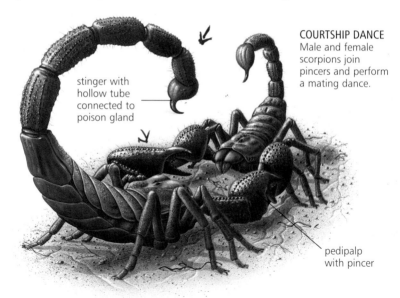

stinger with
hollow tube
connected to
poison gland

COURTSHIP DANCE
Male and female
scorpions join
pincers and perform
a mating dance.

pedipalp
with pincer

BACK HOME
Scorpion eggs hatch inside their mother's body and then emerge as live young. They then climb onto her back.

variable number around the sides. Despite this number, scorpions have poor vision; some species are blind. Instead, scorpions use sensory leg hairs, and a pair of sense organs, called pectines, on the tip of their abdomen, to detect vibrations caused by prey.

SNAPSHOT

ORDER FEATURES **Flattened body; large pedipalps with pincers; segmented abdomen, elongated into a tail tipped with a stinger**
DIET **Insects and other arthropods**
LIFE CYCLE **Eggs hatch inside female's body; nymphs emerge from genital pore**
HABITAT **Under rocks, logs, bark**
DISTRIBUTION **Worldwide**

SCORPIONS, MITES, AND ALLIES 287

SCORPIONES

■ LIFE CYCLE AND DIET
Scorpions have complex mating rituals. A male's pectines sense the pheromone trail left by a female. They interlock pincers to perform a circling dance, during which the male produces a spermatophore. He then maneuvers the female over it so

myn fayret the black
scorplones (1)

IMPERIAL SCORPION
Because daytime temperatures in deserts are so extreme, scorpions venture out to hunt only in the cool of the evening.

STRIKE A POSE
When threatened, this scorpion takes on its classic pose: stinger arched and pincers at the ready .

that she can pick up the packet with her genital pore. The eggs develop and then hatch inside the female's body. The young are born live and climb onto their mother's back. Most species are carried until their first molt about two weeks later; some scorpions take several years to mature.

Scorpions emerge from their daytime retreats at dusk to hunt for insects, spiders, and small vertebrates. They usually crush their victim using their pedipalps; with larger prey they also use their sting. Scorpions cannot ingest solid food. They pour dissolving digestive juices onto the prey's tissues and then suck up the liquid.

■ HABITAT
Scorpions live in dark crevices under bark, stones, or leaf litter, in mainly warm, dry, or humid areas. Some are cave-dwellers.

Pseudoscorpions

Number of species: 3,300

Length: $^1/_{32}$–$^1/_2$ in (1–12 mm)

■ CHARACTERISTICS
These small arachnids, also called false scorpions, are similar in shape to scorpions (Scorpiones), but lack their abdominal tail and stinger. Most species have poison glands in their pincer-like pedipalps. The pedipalps are used to capture prey and in defense. They vary in color from brown and black, to dark green. Pseudoscorpions have up to four eyes, although in some species eyesight is poor or non-existent. They produce nests of silk in burrows for protection when hibernating or molting.

■ LIFE CYCLE AND DIET
Mating and courtship can be complex, sometimes involving a male and female gripping each other by the pedipalps in a courtship dance. Males deposit a spermatophore that is picked up by the female's genital pore. Eggs are laid into a silk sac that is carried under the female's body. In some species, the hatched young cling to their mother's sides; in others, larvae leave the sac and move into soil, bark, or leaf litter.

■ HABITAT
Most species live in warm, humid conditions among leaf litter, bark, and debris. Some live in caves, in birds' nests, the burrows of small mammals, and inside buildings; others live in coastal habitats, in rock crevices, and under stones.

SNAPSHOT

ORDER FEATURES **Flat body; pedipalps with pincer-like claws; oval abdomen with 12 segments**
DIET **Insects, small arthropods**
LIFE CYCLE **Eggs laid in silk sac, carried under female's body**
HABITAT **Among leaf litter, under stones, in caves, birds' nests, and greenhouses**
DISTRIBUTION **Worldwide, except in extreme north, in warm regions**

RIDING HIGH
This rainforest pseudoscorpion is hitching a ride on a harlequin beetle's antenna.

LOADED PINCERS
Most pseudoscorpion species are equipped with venom glands in their pincers.

OPILIONES

40 families

Harvestmen

Number of species: 5,000

Length: 1/16–6 in (2–150 mm)

SNAPSHOT

ORDER FEATURES Long, slender legs; segmented abdomen; pedipalps have six segments
DIET Insects and arthropods
LIFE CYCLE Males transfer sperm via penis; eggs laid in soil
HABITAT Under stones and logs, in debris, leaf litter, and grassy areas
DISTRIBUTION Worldwide, mainly in temperate regions

■ CHARACTERISTICS
Members of this order lack a "waist" between the abdomen and cephalothorax. The pedipalps have six segments and the pincer-like chelicerae have three. The paired eyes are often elevated on small protuberances. Most are dull colored, although some tropical species display bright colors, even changing to blend with their surroundings. Harvestmen have glands in the

REAP THE HARVEST
Most harvestmen are nocturnal hunters. Members of the family Leiobunidae (below) descend from trees to hunt for insects and arthropods on the ground.

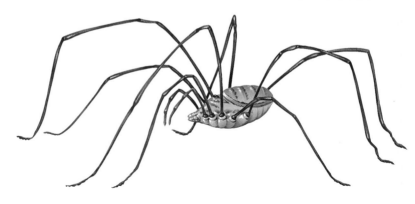

cephalothorax that produce toxic secretions that are smeared on attackers as a deterrent.

SPINY LEGS
This harvestman, a native of Venezuelan cloud forest, has long, sharp spines on its large hindlegs.

■ LIFE CYCLE AND DIET
Unlike other arachnids, male harvestmen have a penis for transferring sperm to the female. Some females have an ovipositor and lay their eggs into crevices in the soil or under bark. In some species, the eggs are laid in damp areas. In one species, the female encloses herself and her young within a mud wall.

■ HABITAT
Harvestmen live among moist debris, under stones and leaf litter, and in caves, usually in grassland and forests. They are found worldwide, mainly in temperate and tropical regions, with the largest number of species concentrated in South America and Southeast Asia.

ACARINA

300 families

Mites and Ticks

Number of species: 30,000

Length: $1/128$–$1\,1/4$ in (0.2–30 mm)

■ CHARACTERISTICS
This huge and diverse order
(known collectively as acarians)
has members with varied habits.
Most acarians are rounded, with
no distinct body division. Their
short abdomen is non-segmented
and the chelicerae are adapted
for piercing and sucking. Adults
and nymphs have four pairs of
walking legs, although larvae
have only three pairs.

■ LIFE CYCLE AND DIET
In some families, males transfer
sperm with their chelicerae.
Acarians lay their eggs wherever
they are feeding: either on plant
material, on food products, in
beehives, in nests and burrows,
or in mattresses, to name a few.
Adults eat a variety of foods,
including plant fluids, blood,
skin, and stored food products.

■ HABITAT
Acarians live in a wide range of
terrestrial and aquatic habitats,
including marine environments.

VELVET UNDERGROUND
Velvet mites emerge from the soil at
certain times of the year to mate and
lay eggs, often after a rain shower.

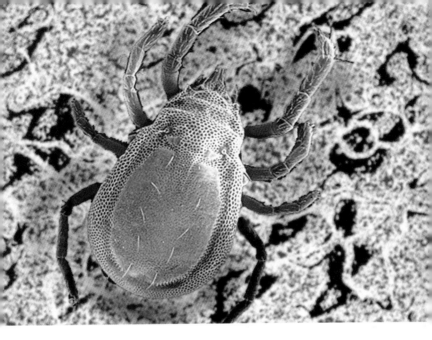

■ MITES

Characteristics There are probably more mite species on Earth than any other arthropod group. Most species are microscopic. Many are translucent, with long abdominal hairs; others are red, orange, green, yellow, or brown, with hairy or spider-like bodies. There is little or no distinction between body parts. They have needle-like chelicerae for sucking blood and plant fluids from host plants or animals.

BIZARRE LIVING
Mites are found in the most unlikely habitats: Some live inside the ears of seals, or inside the lungs of monkeys; others live on the jaws of ants.

Life cycle, diet, and habitat
In some families, males transfer sperm using their chelicerae. Eggs are laid wherever the mites feed. Most have three nymphal stages. Mites are found in almost every terrestrial and aquatic habitat; many are animal parasites.

■ TICKS

Characteristics Ticks are generally larger than mites, especially after a blood meal. Like mites, they have an unsegmented body. Most have three pairs of legs as larvae and four pairs as nymphs and adults. Ticks take in liquid food using their piercing

TICK TOXIN
This microscopic view of a tick shows its piercing mouthparts. Tick saliva contains a toxin that can paralyze some animals.

SHEEP TICK
Hard ticks are serious pests of domestic animals and humans. These sheep ticks attach themselves to a host as it brushes through grass and other vegetation.

and sucking mouthparts. They anchor themselves to a host with a small hook.

Life cycle, diet, and habitat Eggs are laid in the nests and burrows of the hosts, or in vegetation. Most are blood feeders; many species carry diseases.

UROPYGI

2 families

Whipscorpions

Number of species: 99

Length: 3/8–3 in (10–75 mm)

AMBLYPYGI

3 families

Tailless Whipscorpions

Number of species: 130

Length: 3/16–2 1/2 in (5–60 mm)

■ WHIPSCORPIONS

Characteristics Also known as vinegaroons, because of their ability to spray acetic acid from abdominal glands, whipscorpions have a flattened abdomen with 12 segments and a long cephalothorax. The abdomen ends in a whiplike tail. The large and powerful pedipalps, armed with spines, are used to catch and crush prey, and to dig tunnels. Three of the four pairs of legs are used for walking; the first pair have a sensory function.

Life cycle, diet, and habitat A courtship dance precedes mating, where the male places his spermatophore inside the female. The hatched young are carried on her back. They eat insects and other arthropods. They are found in India, Malaysia, and in parts of North and South America, usually in soil, leaf litter, rotting wood, and in caves.

DANCE PARTNERS
Like their relatives the scorpions, male and female whipscorpions lock pincers and perform a courtship dance.

ORDER FEATURES Squat body, large pedipalps with spines, long front legs (Amblypygi); powerful pedipalps, abdomen with whiplike tail (Uropygi)
DIET Insects and other arthropods
LIFE CYCLE Hatched young carried on female's back
HABITAT Leaf litter, under bark
DISTRIBUTION Tropical areas

SAFE AND SOUND
This female tailless whipscorpion, from a Peruvian rainforest, carries the young on her back to protect them from predators.

■ TAILLESS WHIPSCORPIONS
Characteristics Also known as whip-spiders, these squat-bodied arachnids have a broad cephalo-thorax and a flattened abdomen. They have large, sharply spined pedipalps that fold toward the mouth to hold prey. The long first pair of legs are sensory organs.
Life cycle, diet, and habitat Females pick up the spermato-phore deposited by the male. The young develop in a brood sac. They prefer moist areas in leaf litter, caves, and under bark, and are found in tropical areas.

ACID SQUIRT
Whipscorpions do not sting, but instead spray out acetic acid from special glands on their abdomen.

Windscorpions

Number of species: 1,000

Length: 5/32–2³/4 in (4–72 mm)

■ CHARACTERISTICS

Also called sun spiders, these arachnids have a slightly rounded head with huge, forward-facing chelicerae used to kill and slice up prey. Their leg-like pedipalps are without claws, but instead have tiny suction pads that assist in grasping prey. Windscorpions have a segmented, mobile abdomen, small paired eyes, and many sensory body hairs. Most are nocturnal, although some are active during the day.

■ LIFE CYCLE AND DIET

In some families, mating includes males carrying the females. Males place a spermatophore into the female's genital pore. Eggs are laid in burrows in the ground, sometimes in several batches. Most species eat insects and other arthropods, including termites.

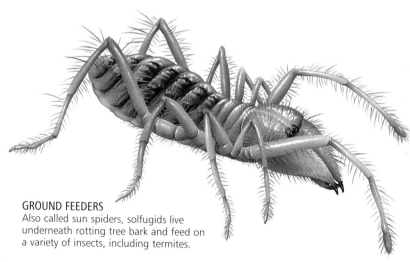

GROUND FEEDERS
Also called sun spiders, solfugids live underneath rotting tree bark and feed on a variety of insects, including termites.

SLICING FANGS
Unlike spiders, solfugids have only one pair of eyes. The sharp, forward-pointing chelicerae are used to macerate prey.

■ HABITAT
Windscorpions live under rocks, on soil, and in leaf litter. They are found mainly in dry areas, including deserts, savanna, and mountainous areas of Central, South, and North America.

SNAPSHOT

ORDER FEATURES Forward-facing chelicerae; leg-like pedipalps
DIET Small insects, mainly termites, and small arthropods
LIFE CYCLE Eggs laid in burrow, in several batches
HABITAT Nocturnal; inside termite colonies; in soil during day
DISTRIBUTION In deserts and mountainous areas of Central, South, and North America

CLASSIFICATION TABLE

The classification of insects and arachnids changes as new knowledge is acquired. Only major orders and families are listed below. Families are listed in alphabetical order. Gaps indicate that the family has no common name.

CLASS INSECTA

ORDER PROTURA   **PROTURANS**
EOSENTOMIDAE

ORDER COLLEMBOLA   **SPRINGTAILS**
ENTOMOBRYIDAE
HYPOGASTRURIDAE
ISOTOMIDAE
ONYCHIURIDAE
SMINTHURIDAE   GLOBULAR SPRINGTAILS

ORDER DIPLURA   **DIPLURANS**
CAMPODEIDAE   CAMPODEIDS
JAPYGIDAE   JAPYGIDS

ORDER ARCHAEOGNATHA   **BRISTLETAILS**
MACHILIDAE   JUMPING BRISTLETAILS
MEINERTELLIDAE

ORDER THYSANURA   **SILVERFISH**
LEPISMATIDAE   SILVERFISH (FIREBRATS)

ORDER EPHEMEROPTERA   **MAYFLIES**
BAETIDAE   SMALL MAYFLIES
EPHEMERELLIDAE   MIDBOREAL MAYFLIES
EPHEMERIDAE   BURROWING MAYFLIES
HEPTAGENIIDAE   STREAM MAYFLIES
LEPTOPHLEBIIDAE   SPINNERS

ORDER ODONATA   **DRAGONFLIES & DAMSELFLIES**
AESCHNIDAE   DARNERS
CALOPTERYGIDAE   BROAD-WINGED DAMSELFLIES
COENAGRIONIDAE   NARROW-WINGED DAMSELFLIES
CORDULEGASTRIDAE   BIDDIES
CORDULIIDAE   GREEN-EYED SKIMMERS
GOMPHIDAE   CLUBTAILS
LESTIDAE   SPREAD-WINGED DAMSELFLIES
LIBELLULIDAE   COMMON SKIMMERS
MACROMIIDAE   BELTED & RIVER SKIMMERS
PETALURIDAE   GRAYBACKS

ORDER BLATTODEA   **COCKROACHES**
BLABERIDAE
BLATTELLIDAE
BLATTIDAE   COMMON COCKROACHES

ORDER MANTODEA   **MANTIDS**
EMPUSIDAE
HYMENOPODIDAE   FLOWER MANTIDS
MANTIDAE   COMMON PRAYING MANTIDS

ORDER ISOPTERA   **TERMITES**
HODOTERMITIDAE   ROTTEN-WOOD TERMITES
KALOTERMITIDAE   DAMP-WOOD TERMITES
MASTOTERMITIDAE
RHINOTERMITIDAE   SUBTERRANEAN TERMITES
TERMITIDAE   NASUTIFORM TERMITES

ORDER ZORAPTERA	**ZORAPTERANS**
ZOROTYPIDAE	ZORAPTERANS
ORDER GRYLLOBLATTODEA	**ICE INSECTS**
GRYLLOBLATTIDAE	ROCK CRAWLERS
ORDER DERMAPTERA	**EARWIGS**
CHELISOCHIDAE	BLACK EARWIGS
FORFICULIDAE	COMMON EARWIGS
LABIDURIDAE	LONG-HORNED EARWIGS
LABIIDAE	LITTLE EARWIGS
ORDER PLECOPTERA	**STONEFLIES**
CAPNIIDAE	SMALL WINTER STONEFLIES
CHLOROPERLIDAE	GREEN STONEFLIES
ISOPERLIDAE	GREEN-WINGED STONEFLIES
LEUCTRIDAE	ROLLED-WINGED STONEFLIES
NEMOURIDAE	SPRING STONEFLIES
PELTOPERLIDAE	ROACHLIKE STONEFLIES
PERLIDAE	COMMON STONEFLIES
PERLODIDAE	PERLODID STONEFLIES
PTERONARCIDAE	GIANT STONEFLIES
TAENIOPTERYGIDAE	WINTER STONEFLIES
ORDER ORTHOPTERA	**GRASSHOPPERS & CRICKETS**
ACRIDIDAE	SHORT-HORNED GRASSHOPPERS
COOLOOLIDAE	COOLOOLA MONSTER
CYLINDRACHETIDAE	SAND GROPERS
ENEOPTERINAE	BUSH CRICKETS
EUMASTACIDAE; TANAOCERIDAE	MONKEY GRASSHOPPERS
GRYLLACRIDIDAE; RHAPHIDOPHORIDAE	LEAF-ROLLING CRICKETS, CAMEL CRICKETS & KIN, CAVE CRICKETS

GRYLLIDAE	TRUE CRICKETS
GRYLLOTALPIDAE	MOLE CRICKETS
MYRMECOPHILIDAE	ANT CRICKETS
OECANTHINAE	TREE CRICKETS
PYRGOMORPHIDAE	
STENOPELMATIDAE	KING CRICKETS
TETRIGIDAE	PYGMY GRASSHOPPERS
TETTIGONIIDAE	LONG-HORNED GRASSHOPPERS & KATYDIDS
TRIDACTYLIDAE	PYGMY MOLE CRICKETS
ORDER PHASMATODEA	**STICK & LEAF INSECTS**
PHASMATIDAE	STICK INSECTS
PHASMIDAE	WALKINGSTICKS
TIMEMIDAE	TIMEMAS
ORDER EMBIOPTERA	**WEBSPINNERS**
CLOTHODIDAE	CLOTHODIDS
EMBIIDAE	EMBIIDS
ORDER PSOCOPTERA	**BOOK LICE & BARK LICE**
LEPIDOPSOCIDAE	SCALY BARKLICE
LIPOSCELIDIDAE	LIPOSCELID BOOKLICE
PSEUDOCAECILIIDAE	
PSOCIDAE	COMMON BARKLICE
PSYLLIPSOCIDAE	PSYLLIPSOCIDS
TROGIIDAE	TROGIID BOOKLICE
ORDER PHTHIRAPTERA	**PARASITIC LICE**
BOOPIDAE	
ECHINOPHTHIRIIDAE	SPINY SUCKING LICE
GYROPIDAE	GUINEA PIG LICE
HAEMATOPINIDAE	MAMMAL-SUCKING LICE
HOPLOPLEURIDAE	
LAEMOBOTHRIIDAE	BIRD LICE

LINOGNATHIDAE	SMOOTH SUCKING LICE
MENOPONIDAE	POULTRY-CHEWING LICE
PEDICULIDAE	HUMAN LICE
PHILOPTERIDAE	FEATHER-CHEWING LICE
RICINIDAE	BIRD LICE
TRICHODECTIDAE	MAMMAL-CHEWING LICE

ORDER HEMIPTERA   BUGS

ACHILIDAE	ACHILID PLANTHOPPERS
ADELGIDAE	PINE APHIDS
ALEYRODIDAE	WHITEFLIES
ALYDIDAE	BROAD-HEADED BUGS
ANTHOCORIDAE	FLOWER BUGS, MINUTE PIRATE BUGS
APHIDIDAE	APHIDS
APHROPHORIDAE	
ARADIDAE	FLAT BUGS, BARK BUGS
ASTEROLECANIIDAE	PIT SCALES
BELOSTOMATIDAE	GIANT WATER BUGS
BERYTIDAE	STILT BUGS
CARSIDARIDAE	
CERCOPIDAE	SPITTLEBUGS & FROGHOPPERS
CHERMIDAE	PINE & SPRUCE APHIDS
CICADELLIDAE	LEAFHOPPERS
CICADIDAE	CICADAS
CIMICIDAE	BED BUGS
CIXIIDAE	CIXIID PLANTHOPPERS
COCCIDAE	SOFT SCALES, WAX SCALES
COLOBATHRISTIDAE	
COREIDAE	LEAF-FOOTED BUGS, CRUSADER BUGS
CORIXIDAE	WATER BOATMEN
CYDNIDAE	NEGRO BUGS
DACTYLOPIIDAE	COCHINEAL BUGS
DELPHACIDAE	DELPHACID PLANTHOPPERS
DERBIDAE	DERBID PLANTHOPPERS
DIASPIDIDAE	ARMORED SCALE INSECTS

DICTYOPHARIDAE	DICTYOPHARID PLANTHOPPERS
DINIDORIDAE	
DIPSOCORIDAE; SCHIZOPTERIDAE	JUMPING GROUND BUGS
ERIOSOMATIDAE	WOOLLY & GALL-MAKING APHIDS
EURYMELIDAE; MEMBRACIDAE	TREEHOPPERS
FLATIDAE	FLATID PLANTHOPPERS
FULGORIDAE	FULGORIDS
GELASTOCORIDAE	TOAD BUGS
GERRIDAE	WATER STRIDERS
HEBRIDAE	VELVET WATER BUGS
HOMOTOMIDAE	
HYDROMETRIDAE	WATER MEASURERS
ISOMETOPIDAE	JUMPING TREE BUGS
ISSIDAE	ISSID PLANTHOPPERS
KERMIDAE	GALL-LIKE COCCIDS
KERRIIDAE; LACCIFERIDAE	LAC INSECTS
LEPTOPODIDAE	SPINY SHORE BUGS
LYGAEIDAE	SEED BUGS
MARGARODIDAE	GIANT SCALE INSECTS
MESOVELIIDAE	WATER TREADERS
MIRIDAE	LEAF OR PLANT BUGS
NABIDAE	DAMSEL BUGS
NAUCORIDAE	CREEPING WATER BUGS
NEPIDAE	WATERSCORPIONS
NOTONECTIDAE	BACKSWIMMERS
OCHTERIDAE	VELVETY SHORE BUGS
ORTHEZIIDAE	ENSIGN SCALES
PELORIDIIDAE	MOSS BUGS
PENTATOMIDAE	STINK BUGS, SHIELD BUGS
PHYLLOXERIDAE	GALL APHIDS
PHYMATIDAE	AMBUSH BUGS
POLYCTENIDAE	BAT BUGS
PSEUDOCOCCIDAE; ERIOCOCCIDAE	MEALYBUGS

PSYLLIDAE	PSYLLIDS, LERPS
PYRRHOCORIDAE	RED BUGS, STAINERS
REDUVIIDAE	ASSASSIN BUGS
RHOPALIDAE	SCENTLESS PLANT BUGS
RICANIIDAE	RICANIID PLANTHOPPERS
SALDIDAE	SHORE BUGS
SCUTELLERIDAE	JEWEL BUGS,
	SHIELD-BACKED BUGS
TESSARATOMIDAE	
TETTIGARCTIDAE	HAIRY CICADAS
TINGIDAE	LACE BUGS
TRIOZIDAE	
VELIIDAE	RIPPLE BUGS

ORDER THYSANOPTERA — **THRIPS**

AEOLOTHRIPIDAE	BANDED THRIPS
PHLOEOTHRIPIDAE	TUBE-TAILED THRIPS
THRIPIDAE	COMMON THRIPS

ORDER MEGALOPTERA — **ALDERFLIES & DOBSONFLIES**

CORYDALIDAE	DOBSONFLIES
SIALIDAE	ALDERFLIES

ORDER RAPHIDIOPTERA — **SNAKEFLIES**

INOCELLIIDAE	
RAPHIDIIDAE	

ORDER NEUROPTERA — **NET-VEINED INSECTS**

ASCALAPHIDAE	OWLFLIES
CHRYSOPIDAE	GREEN LACEWINGS
CONIOPTERYGIDAE	DUSTY-WINGS
HEMEROBIIDAE	BROWN LACEWINGS
ITHONIDAE	MOTH LACEWINGS
MANTISPIDAE	MANTIDFLIES
MYRMELEONTIDAE	ANTLIONS

NEMOPTERIDAE	
POLYSTOECHOTIDAE	GIANT LACEWINGS
PSYCHOPSIDAE	SILKY LACEWINGS
SISYRIDAE	SPONGEFLIES

ORDER COLEOPTERA — **BEETLES**

ANOBIIDAE	FURNITURE BEETLES
ANTHRIBIDAE	FUNGUS WEEVILS
BOSTRICHIDAE	BRANCH & TWIG BORERS, AUGER BEETLES
BRENTIDAE	PRIMITIVE WEEVILS
BRUCHIDAE	SEED BEETLES
BUPRESTIDAE	METALLIC WOOD-BORING BEETLES, JEWEL BEETLES
CANTHARIDAE	SOLDIER BEETLES
CARABIDAE	GROUND BEETLES
CERAMBYCIDAE	LONGHORN BEETLES, LONGICORN BEETLES
CHRYSOMELIDAE	LEAF BEETLES
CICINDELIDAE	TIGER BEETLES
CLERIDAE	CHECKERED BEETLES
COCCINELLIDAE	LADYBIRD BEETLES
CUCUJIDAE	FLAT BARK BEETLES
CURCULIONIDAE	SNOUT BEETLES & WEEVILS
DERMESTIDAE	DERMESTID BEETLES
DYTISCIDAE	PREDACIOUS DIVING BEETLES
ELATERIDAE	CLICK BEETLES
EROTYLIDAE	PLEASING FUNGUS BEETLES
GYRINIDAE	WHIRLIGIG BEETLES
HALIPLIDAE	CRAWLING WATER BEETLES
HISTERIDAE	HISTER BEETLES
HYDROPHILIDAE	WATER SCAVENGER BEETLES
LAEMOPHLOEIDAE	
LAMPYRIDAE	FIREFLIES, LIGHTNING BUGS
LATHRIDIIDAE	MINUTE BROWN SCAVENGER BEETLES
LUCANIDAE	STAG BEETLES

Lycidae	Net-winged beetles
Lymexylidae	Ship-timber beetles
Meloidae	Blister beetles
Melyridae	Softwinged flower beetles
Mycetophagidae	Hairy fungus beetles
Nitidulidae	Nitidulid beetles
Passalidae	Passalid beetles or bessbugs
Psephenidae	Water pennies
Ptiliidae	Feather-winged beetles
Ptinidae	Spider beetles
Pyrochroidae	Fire-colored beetles
Rhipiphoridae	Rhipiphoridan beetles
Scarabaeidae	Scarab beetles
Scolytidae	Bark & ambrosia beetles
Silphidae	Carrion beetles
Silvanidae	Flat grain beetles
Staphylinidae	Rove beetles
Tenebrionidae	Darkling beetles
Trogidae	Carcass beetles
Trogositidae	Bark-gnawing beetles

ORDER STREPSIPTERA TWISTED-WINGED PARASITES

Mengeidae	
Stylopidae	Stylopids

ORDER MECOPTERA SCORPIONFLIES & KIN

Bittacidae	Hangingflies
Boreidae	Snow scorpionflies
Panorpidae	Common scorpionflies

ORDER SIPHONAPTERA FLEAS

Dolichopsyllidae; Ceratophyllidae	Rodent fleas
Leptopsyllidae	Mouse fleas
Pulicidae	Common fleas
Tungidae	Sticktight & chigoe fleas

ORDER DIPTERA FLIES

Acroceridae	Bladder flies
Agromyzidae	Leafminer flies
Anthomyiidae	Anthomyiid flies
Apioceridae	Flower-loving flies
Asilidae	Robber flies
Bibionidae	March flies
Blephariceridae	Net-winged midges
Bombyliidae	Bee flies
Braulidae	Beelice
Calliphoridae	Blowflies
Canacidae	Beach flies
Cecidomyiidae	Gall midges
Ceratopogonidae	Punkies, biting midges
Chaoboridae	Phantom midges
Chironomidae	Midges
Chloropidae	Grass flies
Coelopidae	Seaweed flies
Conopidae	Thick-headed flies
Culicidae	Mosquitoes
Dolichopodidae	Long-legged flies
Drosophilidae	Vinegar (pomace) flies
Empididae	Dance flies, water cruisers
Ephydridae	Shore flies
Fanniidae	
Fergusoninidae	Eucalyptus flies
Heleomyzidae	Sun flies
Hippoboscidae	Louse flies & sheep keds
Lonchaeidae	Lance flies
Micropezidae	Stilt-legged flies
Muscidae	House flies & bushflies
Mycetophilidae	Fungus gnats
Mydidae	Mydas flies
Nemestrinidae	Tanglevein flies

NERRIIDAE	CACTUS FLIES
NEUROCHAETIDAE	UPSIDE-DOWN FLIES
NYCTERIBIIDAE; STREBLIDAE	BAT FLIES
OESTRIDAE; GASTEROPHILIDAE	BOTFLIES
PHORIDAE	SCUTTLE FLIES
PIOPHILIDAE	SKIPPER FLIES
PLATYPEZIDAE	FLAT-FOOTED FLIES
PLATYSTOMATIDAE	PLATYSTOMATID FLIES
PSYCHODIDAE	MOTH FLIES
PTYCHOPTERIDAE	PHANTOM CRANE FLIES
PYRGOTIDAE	PYRGOTID FLIES
RHAGIONIDAE	SNIPE FLIES
SARCOPHAGIDAE	FLESH FLIES
SCENOPINIDAE	WINDOW FLIES
SCIARIDAE	BLACK FUNGUS GNATS
SCIOMYZIDAE	MARCH FLIES
SEPSIDAE	ANT FLIES
SIMULIIDAE	BLACK OR SAND FLIES
SPHAEROCERIDAE	SHORT HEEL FLIES, SMALL DUNG FLIES
STRATIOMYIDAE	SOLDIER FLIES
SYRPHIDAE	HOVER FLIES
TABANIDAE	HORSE & DEER FLIES
TACHINIDAE	TACHINID FLIES
TEPHRITIDAE	FRUIT FLIES
TERATOMYZIDAE	FERN FLIES
THEREVIDAE	STILETTO FLIES
TIPULIDAE	CRANE FLIES
TRICHOCERIDAE	WINTER CRANE FLIES

ORDER TRICHOPTERA   CADDISFLIES

HYDROPSYCHIDAE	NET-SPINNING CADDISFLIES
LEPTOCERIDAE	LONG-HORNED CADDISFLIES
LIMNEPHILIDAE	NORTHERN CADDISFLIES
PHRYGANEIDAE	LARGE CADDISFLIES
PSYCHOMYIIDAE	TUBE-MAKING CADDISFLIES

ORDER LEPIDOPTERA   BUTTERFLIES & MOTHS

ALUCITIDAE	MANY-PLUME MOTHS
ANTHELIDAE	
APATURIDAE	HACKBERRY & GOATWEED BUTTERFLIES
ARCTIIDAE	TIGER MOTHS
BOMBYCIDAE	SILKWORM MOTHS
BUCCULATRICIDAE	
CARPOSINIDAE	CARPOSINID MOTHS
CARTHAEIDAE	
CASTNIIDAE	
CITHERONIIDAE	ROYAL MOTHS
COLEOPHORIDAE	CASEBEARER MOTHS
COSMOPTERYGIDAE	
COPROMORPHIDAE	
COSSIDAE	WOOD MOTHS
CTENUCHIDAE	CTENUCHID MOTHS
DANAIDAE	MILKWEED BUTTERFLIES
DREPANIDAE	HOOK-TIP MOTHS
EUPTEROTIDAE; ZANOLIDAE	ZANOLID MOTHS
GELECHIIDAE	GELECHIID MOTHS
GEOMETRIDAE	MEASURINGWORM MOTHS, LOOPERS
GRACILARIIDAE	LEAF BLOTCH MINERS
HEPIALIDAE	GHOST MOTHS, SWIFTS
HESPERIIDAE	SKIPPERS
INCURVARIIDAE	YUCCA MOTHS & KIN
LASIOCAMPIDAE	TENT CATERPILLAR & LAPPET MOTHS
LIBYTHEIDAE	SNOUT BUTTERFLIES
LIMACODIDAE	
LYCAENIDAE	GOSSAMER-WINGED BUTTERFLIES
LYMANTRIIDAE	TUSSOCK MOTHS & KIN
LYONETIIDAE	LYONETIID MOTHS
NOCTUIDAE	NOCTUIDS

NOTODONTIDAE	PROMINENTS
NYMPHALIDAE	BRUSH-FOOTS
OECOPHORIDAE	OECOPHORID MOTHS
PAPILIONIDAE	SWALLOWTAILS & KIN
PIERIDAE	WHITES & SULFURS
PLUTELLIDAE	DIAMONDBACK MOTHS
PTEROPHORIDAE	PLUME MOTHS
PSYCHIDAE	BAGWORM MOTHS
PYRALIDAE	PYRALID MOTHS
RIODINIDAE	METALMARKS
SATURNIIDAE	GIANT SILKWORM MOTHS
SATYRIDAE	SATYRS, NYMPHS, & ARCTICS
SESIIDAE	CLEAR-WINGED MOTHS
SPHINGIDAE	SPHINX OR HAWK MOTHS
THAUMETOPOEIDAE	
TINEIDAE	CLOTHES MOTHS & KIN
TORTRICIDAE	TORTRICID MOTHS
URANIIDAE	
YPONOMEUTIDAE	ERMINE MOTHS
ZYGAENIDAE	SMOKY MOTHS

ORDER HYMENOPTERA — BEES, ANTS, WASPS, & SAWFLIES

AGAONIDAE	FIG WASPS
ANDRENIDAE	ANDRENID BEES
APIDAE	DIGGER BEES, CARPENTER BEES, CUCKOO BEES, BUMBLEBEES, HONEYBEES & KIN
ARGIDAE	ARGID SAWFLIES
BRACONIDAE	BRACONIDS
CEPHIDAE	STEM SAWFLIES
CHALCIDIDAE	CHALCIDS
CHRYSIDIDAE	CUCKOO WASPS
CIMBICIDAE	CIMBICID SAWFLIES
COLLETIDAE	YELLOW-FACED & PLASTERER BEES

CYNIPIDAE	GALL WASPS
ENCYRTIDAE	ENCYRTID WASPS
EULOPHIDAE; APHELININAE	EULOPHID WASPS
EURYTOMIDAE	SEED CHALCIDS
EVANIIDAE	HATCHET WASPS
FORMICIDAE	ANTS
HALICTIDAE	SWEAT (HALICTID) BEES
IBALIIDAE	IBALIID WASPS
ICHNEUMONIDAE	ICHNEUMONIDS
MEGACHILIDAE	LEAF-CUTTING BEES
MELITTIDAE	MELITTID BEES
MUTILLIDAE	VELVET ANTS
MYMARIDAE	FAIRY WASPS
PELECINIDAE	PELECINIDS
PERGIDAE	PERGID SAWFLIES
POMPILIDAE	SPIDER WASPS
PTEROMALIDAE	PTEROMALID WASPS
SCELIONIDAE	SCELIONID WASPS
SCOLIIDAE	SCOLIID WASPS
SIRICIDAE	HORNTAILS
SPHECIDAE	SPHECID WASPS
STEPHANIDAE	STEPHANID WASPS
SYMPHYTA	SAWFLIES
TENTHREDINIDAE	COMMON SAWFLIES
TIPHIIDAE	TIPHID WASPS
TORYMIDAE	TORYMID WASPS
VESPIDAE	VESPID WASPS

CLASS ARACHNIDA

ORDER ARANEAE — SPIDERS

AGELENIDAE	FUNNEL WEAVERS
ANTRODIAETIDAE	FOLDING TRAPDOOR SPIDERS
ARANEIDAE	ORB WEAVERS
CLUBIONIDAE	SAC SPIDERS
CTENIDAE	WANDERING SPIDERS
CTENIZIDAE	TRAPDOOR SPIDERS
DICTYNIDAE	DICTYNID SPIDERS
DIPLURIDAE	FUNNEL-WEB SPIDERS
ERESIDAE	ERESID SPIDERS
HETEROPODIDAE	HUNTSMAN SPIDERS
LINYPHIIDAE	DWARF SPIDERS
LOXOSCELIDAE	VIOLIN SPIDERS
LYCOSIDAE	WOLF SPIDERS
OXYOPIDAE	LYNX SPIDERS
PHOLCIDAE	DADDY-LONG-LEGS SPIDERS
PISAURIDAE	NURSERY-WEB SPIDERS
SALTICIDAE	JUMPING SPIDERS
SCYTODIDAE	SPITTING SPIDERS
SELENOPIDAE	SELENOPID CRAB SPIDERS
SPARASSIDAE	GIANT CRAB SPIDERS
TETRAGNATHIDAE	LARGE-JAWED ORB WEAVERS
THERAPHOSIDAE	TARANTULAS
THERIDIIDAE	COMB-FOOTED SPIDERS
THOMISIDAE	CRAB SPIDERS

ORDER SCORPIONES — SCORPIONS

BUTHIDAE	BUTHID SCORPIONS
IURIDAE	IURID SCORPIONS

ORDER PSEUDOSCORPIONES — PSEUDO-SCORPIONS

CHELIFERIDAE	
CHERNETIDAE	CHERNETIDS

ORDER OPILIONES — HARVESTMEN

LEIOBUNIDAE	
PHALANGIIDAE	

ORDER ACARINA — MITES & TICKS

ARGASIDAE	SOFT TICKS
HYDRACHNELLAE	WATER MITES
IXODIDAE	HARD TICKS
TETRANYCHIDAE	SPIDER MITES
TROMBIDIIDAE	VELVET MITES

ORDER UROPYGI — WHIPSCORPIONS

THELYPHONIDAE	VINEGAROONS

ORDER AMBLYPYGI — TAILLESS WHIPSCORPIONS

PHRYNIDAE	
TARANTULIDAE	

ORDER SOLIFUGAE — WINDSCORPIONS

EREMOBATIDAE	
SOLPUGIDAE	

GLOSSARY

Abdomen The rear part of an insect's or spider's body. It holds the digestive, respiratory, and reproductive system organs.

Antenna (*pl.* antennae) A delicate, mobile sense organ on an insect's head; antennae respond to smell, touch, or taste.

Arachnid An arthropod with four pairs of walking legs, a body divided into two parts (the cephalothorax and abdomen), chelicerae, and simple eyes.

Arthropod An animal with jointed limbs and a body divided into segments covered by a tough exoskeleton.

Caste A specialized group within a social colony that carries out certain specific tasks.

Cephalothorax The head and thorax of an arachnid, fused into one body segment.

Cercus (*pl.* cerci) One of a pair of tail-like, sensory extensions on the end of the abdomen of some insects.

Chelicera (*pl.* chelicerae) Pincer-like or fang-like biting appendages on the cephalothorax of arachnids.

Chitin A hard, flexible substance that gives an exoskeleton its strength.

Chrysalis The pupa of a butterfly.

Cocoon A silken case made by the fully grown larva of many insects; in some adult insects and spiders, a protective case for themselves and their eggs.

Complete metamorphosis *See* **Metamorphosis**

Compound eye An insect's main pair of eyes, made up of many smaller eyes, or lenses, each one of which detects movement separately.

Cuticle *See* **Exoskeleton**

Drone A male honeybee that mates with a young queen.

Ecosystem A community or network of living things and their interactions with their environment.

Ectoparasite A parasite that lives on the outside of a host's body, feeding on it without killing it.

Egg sac A silk covering woven by some female spiders to protect their eggs.

Elytron (*pl.* elytra) The hard, rigid forewing of a beetle that covers and protects the delicate flying wing underneath.

Endoparasite A parasite that lives on the inside of a host, feeding on it but not killing it.

Exoskeleton The hard, protective structure covering the body of an arthropod. It is made of chitin, and it supports the muscles and soft internal organs. Also called the cuticle.

Eyespot A round, eye-like marking on the wings of certain insects.

Furcula The forked organ on the abdomen of springtails, used for jumping.

Grub The legless larva of an ant, bee, wasp, or beetle.

Haltere One of a pair of small, knob-like structures in flies, which act as stabilizers during flight, and modified hindwings.

Honeydew A sweet liquid, rich in carbohydrates, produced by sap-feeding insects, such as aphids.

Host An animal that is attacked by a parasite.

Incomplete metamorphosis *See* **Metamorphosis**

Larva (*pl.* larvae) The immature stage of an insect that undergoes complete metamorphosis to become an adult.

Maggot The legless larva of some flies.

Mandibles The biting jaws of an insect.

Metamorphosis The transformation of an immature insect into an adult through a series of stages. Some insects develop by complete metamorphosis, where the young (larvae) look very different to the adults. Other insects develop by incomplete metamorphosis, where the young (nymphs) look like small versions of the adults.

Mimicry When an animal copies or imitates the coloration, patterning, or behavioral characteristics of another animal in order to maximize its survival.

Molt The process of shedding an outer layer of the body (the exoskeleton).

Nymph The immature stage of an insect that develops by gradual or incomplete metamorphosis to become an adult. Nymphs are often similar to adults, but do not have fully developed wings.

Ocellus (*pl.* ocelli) A simple, light-sensitive organ on the top of the head of many insects. Insects usually have three ocelli.

Order A large group of related plants or animals. An order is divided into smaller groups, from suborders, families, and genera, down to species.

Ovipositor A tube at the tip of a female insect's abdomen used for laying eggs.

Parasite A species that lives on or feeds off the body tissues of another species (called a host), usually without killing it.

Pedipalps A pair of appendages at the front of the cephalothorax of some arachnids, used to touch, taste, and smell; male spiders use modified pedipalps to transfer sperm to the female.

Pheromone A chemical message or signal, used by many animals to communicate, usually with the same species.

Predator An animal that hunts or preys on other animals for its food.

Proboscis A tube-like mouthpart used by certain insects for sucking food.

Proleg The unsegmented leg on a larval insect.

Pronotum The dorsal covering over the first segment of the thorax.

Pupa The stage in development that an insect undergoes to finish complete metamorphosis. Inside a tough pupal case, it changes dramatically as its juvenile body parts break down and adult features emerge.

Rostrum The sucking mouthparts of bugs, or the lengthened part of the head of weevils.

Spinnerets Two to six finger-like organs at the tip of a spider's abdomen. Various types of silk made by the spider emerge from the spinnerets.

Spigots Tubes that spin spider silk into strands.

Spiracles The breathing holes in the side of an insect that take oxygen into the body and expel waste gases, such as carbon dioxide.

Stinger A hollow structure on the tail of insects (Order Hymenoptera) and scorpions that pierces flesh and injects venom.

Telson The final segment of the abdomen of some arachnids.

Thorax The middle section of an insect's body, to which the legs and wings are attached.

Vestigial Describing the reduced size or simplified function of an organ during the progress of evolution of a species.

INDEX

Page numbers in *italics* indicate illustrations and photos

ACKNOWLEDGMENTS

[t = top, b = bottom, l = left, r = right, c = center, F = Front, C = Cover, B = Back]

Picture Credits

All photographs by Corel except for:

K. Atkinson 214b. **Auscape** 111b (V. Steger/P. Arnold); 119t (K. Atkinson); 60b (D. Bringard/Bios); 295 (B.S.I.P.); 287t (J. Cancalosi); 149b, 163c (D. Clyne); 179t (J. P. Ferrero); 75t, 113t, 150t, 155t, 192b, 206c (P. Geotgheluck); 219t (G. Harold); 64tr (C. A. Henley); 109t (H. Van Ingen); 31c, 48t, 90t, 265t (M. Macconacchie); 34cr, 65tl, 133t, 251c (R. Morrison); 121l (F. Polking); 261 (A. & J. Six); 230b (S. Wilby & C. Ciantar). **APL** 42r, 112b (Corbis). **Bruce Coleman** 58b (J. Burton); 183t (J. Cancalosi); 68b (G. Dore); 26b (F. Labhardt); 26t (Dr. F. Sauer); 26b (A. Stillwell); 64tc, 64bl, 65tc, 126–127c, 210t, 249b (K. Taylor); 261b (M. P. L. Fogden); 71b (P. Zabransky); 249b. **Corbis** 106c; 115c. **Hemera Studio** 93c, 139c, 141c, 142b, 144c, 147t, 149t, 157c, 159c, 164c, 165t, 165b, 181c, 191t, 195, 236b, 237b, 238b, 239t, 241t, 242b, 243t, 244b, 246b, 247t, 249t, 263t, 269c, 277t, 281c. **NHM Picture Library** 205t. **Oxford Scientific Films** 202t (N. Bromhall); 4–5r, 32b, 33c, 175t (M. Fogden); 279t (S. Kuribayashi); 55c, 222b, 297c (London Scientific Films); 153t, 282b (S. Morris); 43c (P. de Oliveira); 40cl (J. H. Robinson); 167t. PhotoDisc 245c, 268c, 283t. **photolibrary.com** 114b (W. Ervin/SPL); 120b (A. Evrard); 2c (S. Holt); 296b (K. H. Kjeldsen/SPL); 6–7c, 9–10c (Nurdsany & Perennou/SPL); 40t (D. Scharf/SPL); 174b, 210b, 259t (D. Scharf/SPL); 169t (SPL); 155b (A. Syred/SPL); 192l; 215t; 278b. **Planet Earth Pictures** 179b, 246t (B. Kenney); 173b (K. Lucas); 257c (D. P. Maitland). **Premaphotos Wildlife** 272b (R. Brown); 104–105c; 40b, 77t, 99t, 133b, 143b, 145c, 146b, 162b, 168b, 170b, 171t, 172b, 180b, 184b, 185t, 186b, 187t, 209c, 213t, 220t, 229c, 253t, 255c, 264b, 265b, 291b, 298b, 301t (K. Preston-Mafham); 190b (J. Preston-Mafham); 131c, 135t, 188-189t, 197t, 223t, 299b (Dr. R. Preston-Mafham). **Science Gallery** 107c, 111t (O.S.F./Auscape). **Stock Photos** 40l. **Tom Stack & Associates** 176b (D. M. Dennis).

Illustration Credits

Susanna Addario 95b, 198. **Anne Bowman** 1, 15b, 54, 76tr, 86b, 89cr, 89tr, 280. **Martin Camm** 116, 122. **Sandra Doyle/Wildlife Art** 12, 18t, 19, 29, 39b, 40t, 52br, 59, 178, 202, 260, 270, 271, 276. **Simone End** 3, 38bl, 48b, 49b, 85, 105, 193, 195. **Christer Eriksson** 30, 45b, 62b, 79b, 158, 196, 286. **Alan Ewart** 83. **Giuliano Fornari** 52bl, 80b, 80t, 81b. **Jon Gittoes** 177. **Ray Grinaway** 21, 34, 39t, 44, 45, 45cl, 45tc, 45tl, 45tr, 46cr, 76tl, 82br, 89tl, 96, 121, 161, 212, 218, 220, 221, 224, 231, 232, 250, 275, 279. **Tim Hayward/ Bernard Thornton Artists UK** 65b, 65cr, 72, 103. **Robert Hynes** 66, 67b, 67t. **Ian Jackson/Wildlife Art** 197. **Cathy Johnson** 176, 227. **David Kirshner** 17bc, 17bl, 17br, 23, 44b, 130, 135b. **Frank Knight** 70t, 203, 227. **Angela Lober** 74, 162. **John Mac/ FOLIO** 56. **Rob Mancini** 9, 24br, 25b, 27, 54, 228, 233, 260, 267, 292, 300. **Iain McKellar** 36. **James McKinnon** 34, 42, 86t, 87, 182, 194, 236, 254, 256. **Nicola Oram** 101b, 240. **Tony Pyrzakowski** 102. **John Richards** 57b, 200, 201. **Edwina Riddell** 95t. **Steve Roberts/Wildlife Art** 88b, 125b, 204, 206, 207, 232, 235, 248, 252, 262. **Trevor Ruth** 47, 225. **Claudia Saraceni** 28, 108r, 110, 215. **Chris Shields/Wildlife Art** 57t, 82b, 94, 151b, 256, 274, 283. **Kevin Stead** 38br, 50l, 51, 69, 79t, 98, 99b, 100, 108t, 108l, 118, 127, 146, 154, 197, 199, 223, 234, 258, 259. **Thomas Trojer** 16b. **Genevieve Wallace** 148, 160, 241.

The publishers wish to thank Sarah Anderson, Kate Brady, Megan Wardle, and Puddingburn Publishing Services for their help in the preparation of this book.